UNDERSTANDING TRACY LETTS

UNDERSTANDING CONTEMPORARY AMERICAN LITERATURE
Matthew J. Bruccoli, Founding Editor
Linda Wagner-Martin, Series Editor

Also of Interest

UNDERSTANDING

TRACY LETTS

Thomas Fahy

THE UNIVERSITY OF
SOUTH CAROLINA PRESS

Published by the University of South Carolina Press
Columbia, South Carolina 29208

www.uscpress.com

Manufactured in the United States of America

29 28 27 26 25 24 23 22 21 20
10 9 8 7 6 5 4 3 2 1

Library of Congress Cataloging-in-Publication Data
can be found at http://catalog.loc.gov/.

ISBN 978-1-64336-110-9 (hardback)
ISBN 978-1-64336-111-6 (paperback)
ISBN 978-1-64336-112-3 (ebook)

A version of Chapter 4 was first published in *Modern Drama,*
2020, Volume 63, Number 2. Reprinted with permission from
University of Toronto Press (https://utpjournals.press).

A version of Chapter 3 was first published as an article in the
Popular Culture Studies Journal, 2019, Volume 7, Number 2.

For Kimball

CONTENTS

SERIES EDITOR'S PREFACE

The Understanding Contemporary American Literature series was founded by the estimable Matthew J. Bruccoli (1931–2008), who envisioned these volumes as guides or companions for students as well as good nonacademic readers, a legacy that will continue as new volumes are developed to fill in gaps among the nearly one hundred series volumes published to date and to embrace a host of new writers only now making their marks on our literature.

As Professor Bruccoli explained in his preface to the volumes he edited, because much influential contemporary literature makes special demands, "the word *understanding* in the titles was chosen deliberately. Many willing readers lack an adequate understanding of how contemporary literature works; that is, of what the author is attempting to express and the means by which it is conveyed." Aimed at fostering this understanding of good literature and good writers, the criticism and analysis in the series provide instruction in how to read certain contemporary writers—explicating their material, language, structures, themes, and perspectives—and facilitate a more profitable experience of the works under discussion.

In the twenty-first century Professor Bruccoli's prescience gives us an avenue to publish expert critiques of significant contemporary American writing. The series continues to map the literary landscape and to provide both instruction and enjoyment. Future volumes will seek to introduce new voices alongside canonized favorites, to chronicle the changing literature of our times, and to remain, as Professor Bruccoli conceived, contemporary in the best sense of the word.

Linda Wagner-Martin, Series Editor

ACKNOWLEDGMENTS

I want to thank Linda Wagner-Martin for her support of this project and so many others. I am also grateful to the University of South Carolina Press, to the readers at *Modern Drama, The Journal of Popular Culture,* and the *Popular Culture Studies Journal,* to my inspirational colleagues at Long Island University, and to James MacDonald for sharing his insights on the theater with me over the years.

To my family and friends, no project is possible without you—especially Tatyana Tsinberg and my son Nicolai, who experienced his first Broadway play this year. I hope the arts continue to captivate and inspire you.

Last, I wish to dedicate this book to the memory of Kimball King. Kimball gave me my first opportunity to write about the theater. He was always kind, generous, and quick with a witty story and a smile. He will be missed.

CHAPTER 1

Understanding Tracy Letts

"I try to be upbeat and funny. Everybody in
Tracy's stories gets naked or dead."

Billie Letts

Experiencing a Tracy Letts play often feels akin to reading a Cormac McCarthy novel, watching a Cohen Brothers film, and seeing an episode of *Breaking Bad* at the same time. His characters can be ruthlessly cruel and funny, selfish and generous, delusional and incisive, deceptive and painfully honest. They keep secrets. They harbor biases and misconceptions. And in their quest to find love and understanding, they often end up being the greatest impediments to their own happiness. As a writer, Letts can move seamlessly from the milieu of a Texas trailer park to the pulsating nightlife of London's countercultural scene, from the stifling quiet of small-town Ohio to the racial tensions of urban Chicago. He thrives in the one-act format, like *Mary Page Marlowe* and *The Minutes,* as well as the epic scope of *August: Osage County* and *Linda Vista*. With a musician's sense for timing, he shifts between humor and heartache, silence and sound, and the mundane and the poetic. And he fearlessly tackles issues such as gender bias, racism, homophobia, and disability rights. Contemporary American life thus becomes a way to comment on the country's troubled history, from Native American genocide to the civil rights movement. In this way, the personal narratives of his characters become gateways to the political.

Born in Tulsa, Oklahoma, in 1965, Letts grew up in the small town of Durant. Home of the "World's Largest Peanut" monument and an annual magnolia festival, Durant did not offer many artistic outlets for him. His parents, Billie and Dennis Letts, were both English professors at Southeastern Oklahoma State University, but they retired early to pursue other careers. Billie became a novelist, and her first effort, *Where the Heart Is* (1995), landed on the bestseller list after Oprah Winfrey selected it for her book club a few years later. For Dennis, acting began as a pastime at the university and extended into community theater. His success landed him roles in nearly fifty films, including the adaptation of his wife's first novel. Not surprisingly, the Letts house was filled with books, and Tracy's parents encouraged his interest in the arts—whether helping him stage his own plays or introducing him to music, theater, and film. Dennis, for example, took his son to see the Rolling Stones at the age of four and introduced him to jazz at six. In the same year, Tracy penned "The Psychopath," a short story about a man who hangs and shoots himself at the same time. Though his first grade teacher gave him an "A++" for the assignment, his mother wondered in retrospect why the school didn't call social services.[1] A few years later, Dennis brought him to one of his performances as Atticus Finch in *To Kill a Mockingbird,* and around that time Tracy got his first taste of movie magic. Going to the drive-in with his grandfather and brother made an indelible impression on him. It was film that introduced him to some of the masterpieces of American theater after all, including *Who's Afraid of Virginia Woolf* (Bigsby, *Twenty-First,* 93). Outside of the home, however, the town of Durant was defined largely by conservative Christian politics and casual racism. The police once evicted the Letts family after Billie had tea with a black woman on their front porch, and Letts recalls daily reminders of prejudice: "I don't remember a day going by at school when I didn't hear someone railing on black people or devil worshipers. We had as many black people as we had devil worshipers in Durant, meaning none."[2]

When Tracy was ten years old, his grandfather committed suicide by drowning, and this death precipitated his grandmother's descent into substance abuse. She spent years in and out of detox centers and psychiatric wards, smuggling in pills through any means possible. Billie once insisted that Tracy film his grandmother going through a "downer delirium." As he explains, "it's the creepiest three minutes you have ever seen. Not particularly dramatic, just depressing." While these events would later become the basis for his Pulitzer Prize–winning play *August: Osage County,* they also raised the specter of addiction for Tracy. His mother soon became an alcoholic, describing drinking as a "beast . . . just waiting" inside of her. After an incident in which Dennis felt publicly humiliated by her behavior, however, she started attending Alcoholics Anonymous.[3] The title character from *Mary Page Marlowe* and Anita in *Linda Vista* would follow the same path from addiction to recovery—as would Tracy himself. In high school, he started drinking and doing drugs, including freebase cocaine.

Bullied and unpopular as a teenager, Letts could not wait to get out of Oklahoma. In 1983, the eighteen-year-old moved to the nearest big city, Dallas, to pursue acting, but he did not find much of a theater community there.[4] Two years later he relocated to Chicago. One of his earliest opportunities came from the Steppenwolf Theatre Company's outreach program for children where he appeared in a production of *The Glass Menagerie* for $25 a show. Steppenwolf, a dynamic non-profit theater company that opened in 1974, produced cutting-edge contemporary works. Its collaborative ethos, inviting members to act, direct, design, and write, would eventually become central to Letts's approach to playwriting. At the time, however, he just wanted to pay the bills. While struggling to find steady work as an actor, holding down a nine-to-five job as a secretary, and drinking heavily, Letts began writing his first play in the late eighties and early nineties. He channeled much of his anger and frustration at the time into it. He remembers coming to work hungover nearly every day, trying to revise the mess he had written the night before. Eventually he submitted an early draft of *Killer Joe* to the Illinois Arts Council in the hopes of securing a grant. He also started to arrange readings, but the reaction among fellow actors was not what he had hoped. Some "people burst into tears and walked out. Not for good reasons either." Even his parents told him that no one would ever produce it. A few months later, unemployed and broke, buying American Airlines frozen dinners with his girlfriend's food stamps, he received a letter awarding him $5,000 from the Arts Council.[5]

Initially, Steppenwolf had no interest in the play. As Letts recalls, "I gave her [director Anna D. Shapiro] *Killer Joe* at one point, and she hated it."[6] It took Letts a couple of years to get the play produced, and it premiered with the Next Theatre Lab on August 3, 1993 in Evanston, Illinois. This production was a turning point for him. Twenty-four days later, Letts got sober and landed his first major role in Steve Martin's *Picasso at Lapin Agile,* which ran for 468 performances (Mayer 104–5). Steppenwolf also started to take an interest in *Killer Joe,* raising funds to produce it at the Edinburgh Festival in Scotland, and Martin donated $5,000 to support the effort. Set in a trailer park, *Killer Joe* tells the story of a working-poor Texas family that lies, cheats, drinks, sells drugs, and plots the mother's murder for her life insurance policy. The title refers to Joe Cooper, the detective and gun-for-hire who uses Chris's sister, Dottie, as a sexual "retainer" for the killing. Literal and moral poverty defines the lives of these characters, shaping their choices and driving them to exploit each other with impunity.

Letts's subsequent play *Bug,* which premiered in London in 1996, uses a seedy motel on the outskirts of Oklahoma City to capture a similar snapshot of American life. It focuses on a woman, Agnes White, who remains emotionally paralyzed by the disappearance of her son ten years earlier. Freebasing cocaine and drinking heavily only dull the pain, for she cannot escape reminders of her lost child. When she meets Peter, an AWOL soldier convinced that he is the subject of a secret government experiment to breed bugs, she embraces his delusions to make sense of the tragedy in her life. Letts explores the appeal of and problems with conspiracy theories through Agnes's descent into Peter's madness. Marginalized by poverty, pain, and paranoia, these characters desperately want "to make a connection," and conspiracy gives them a sense of significance. It elevates them from being the invisible poor to lynchpins in a government plot. At the same time, such conspiracies undermine the kind of social action necessary to change the conditions trapping Agnes and Peter in the first place. They deflect attention from the class hierarchies that leave so many at the bottom, and the extreme violence of the play's ending, with Agnes and Peter burning themselves to death, presents systemic poverty as unsustainable and dangerous for the country as a whole.

In 1997, Letts moved to Los Angeles with his partner, actress Holly Wantuch, who starred in the original production of *Killer Joe*. She died from a stroke shortly after the move, but Letts remained on the West Coast for a few years, securing small roles in films and television shows such as *Seinfeld, Profiler,* and *Strong Medicine*. He returned to Chicago and became an official member of Steppenwolf in 2001. The rest of his plays would be written explicitly for that ensemble. *Man from Nebraska*, a finalist for the Pulitzer Prize in 2004, departs from his earlier work in tone and scope. Letts abandons the emotionally destabilized, impoverished worlds of the Smith family and Agnes White for Ken Carpenter, a fifty-seven-year old family man who travels to London after losing his faith in God. Though Ken's middle-class suburban life shows no trace of the violence and paranoia found in *Killer Joe* and *Bug*, it shares some of the claustrophobia. His life in Lincoln, with its routines of marriage, work, and churchgoing, have begun to suffocate Ken. When he announces to his wife that he no longer believes in God, she asks, "How can something that was there yesterday not be there today?" (17). This question encapsulates the play's central exploration of loss. Just as one can lose religious faith, marriages can fray. Children can become emotionally distant. And parents die. For the first time, Ken recognizes life as fragile and ephemeral. His subsequent trip to London gives him a glimpse into economic hardships and ethnic divisions absent from suburban Nebraska. It also introduces him to art, and Ken's sculpting lessons become a way for him to bridge some of these differences and to heal the broken bonds in his family.

While Letts continued his work as an actor with Steppenwolf, the off-Broadway premiere of *Bug* in 2004 offered another glimpse into his creative process. This revival, like the previous productions in Washington, D.C., in 2000 and Chicago in 2001, enabled Letts to reshape the material. As he explains, "The play wasn't worked out. It took a long time and a lot of productions for me to work out some of the problems with it."[7] This process of revision certainly resonates with his own approach to writing and the ethos of Steppenwolf. As a writer, Letts prefers to hammer out first drafts on an IBM Selectric typewriter before copying them onto a computer, printing them out, and deleting the file. This final step "forces him to retype—and rewrite—as he goes" (McKinley). Steppenwolf also views revision as essential to any production. According to John Mayer, this group has "a deep connection to the process of new play development" (181), and it views drama as a collaborative art. Letts has acknowledged the importance of this creative community for his own work: "My plays here [at Steppenwolf] are prodded, tested, questioned by people who are—they're all very well-versed in interrogating a new play."[8] This environment proved crucial for both *Bug* and his next work, *August: Osage County*. Director and ensemble member Anna D. Shapiro remembers reading the latter for the first time: "It was only the first two acts and a sketch of a third act . . . I couldn't put it down . . . It needed a lot of work, because it was so big. But, obviously we were going to do it."[9] Letts's intimate knowledge of the Steppenwolf actors, directors, and set designers helped him craft the personal subject matter of this play into a masterpiece about family in a nation defined by class and racial divisions.

The play opens with the drowning suicide of Beverly Weston, an academic and poet who has watched his career decline, his health deteriorate due to alcoholism, and his family grow apart. The rancorous relationship with his pill-addicted wife, Violet, only exacerbates the dusty oppressiveness of their lives together. For both Beverly and his eldest daughter Barbara, the family's deterioration becomes a metaphor for the nation as a whole: "This country, this experiment, America . . . what a lament if no one saw it go" (91). As their last name suggests, the Weston family evokes the promise of the frontier, but this promise has not come to fruition for them. Barbara's marriage is over. Her other sisters appear to be in doomed relationships as well. Ivy, whose cervical cancer has left her barren, does not realize that she has been dating her half-brother, and Karen's fiancé tries to sexually assault Barbara's fourteen-year-old daughter. By setting the play in Oklahoma, at the end of the Trail of Tears, Letts also suggests that the country's history of colonial oppression remains a corrupting force. The only person capable of sustained caretaking is the Cheyenne housekeeper Johnna, and she does so because poverty gives her no other option.

After the critically acclaimed, sold-out run at Steppenwolf in 2007, the New York premiere garnered similar enthusiasm for this epic, three-and-a-half-hour play. Charles Isherwood for the *New York Times* described it as "the most exciting new American play Broadway has seen in years," and the *New York*

Post characterized the staging and acting as "simply beautiful."[10] The unexpected thrill of this success was marred by tragic news, however. Between the two productions, Letts's father was diagnosed with Stage IV lung cancer. "It was a terrible time in my life and made all the more terrible by how great this other part of my life was," Letts recalls.[11] Dennis, who had been cast as Beverly Weston, performed the role as long as he could, but he died shortly into the New York run—six weeks before his son won the Pulitzer Prize in 2008.

Letts followed the emotional rollercoaster of *August: Osage County* with something lighter, yet the 2008 comedy *Superior Donuts* offers a meditation on some of the same socioeconomic clashes evident in his earlier works. Comedy can be deceptive in Letts. It often becomes the vehicle for some of his most pointed cultural commentary. As he explains, "if they're laughing, they're listening, and I want them to listen."[12] The humor in *Superior Donuts* becomes a way to examine the racial and economic tensions of modern-day America. Set in a failing donut shop in Uptown Chicago, owner Arthur Przybyszewski has withdrawn from the world. His estranged wife has just died of cancer. He hasn't seen his fifteen-year-old daughter in five years. And he seems unconcerned with the store's decline. After hiring Franco Wicks, a vivacious African American man, Arthur finds himself questioning his choices to evade the draft during the Vietnam War and to abandon his commitment to social justice. From Franco's commentary about racism to Arthur's passion for African American poetry, the play highlights the need for building communities founded on the principles of fairness and empathy. When a bookie harms Franco and destroys his manuscript for *America Will Be,* Arthur pays the debt and takes on the role of surrogate father, helping Franco rewrite the novel. As its title suggests, the promise of America has yet to be realized, and Arthur and Franco become a model for doing so.

It would be several years before Letts's next original play, but he continued to write while his acting career flourished. In 2011, he collaborated with director William Friedkin for the film version of *Killer Joe,*[13] and he penned a stage adaptation of Anton Chekhov's *Three Sisters* for Steppenwolf in the summer of 2012. The following year would prove a watershed for Letts—both professionally and personally. Meryl Streep and Julia Roberts starred in the film *August: Osage County* with Letts writing the screenplay. He joined the cast of the television series *Homeland* in the recurring role of Andrew Lockhart. And his Broadway debut as an actor earned him a Tony for his performance as George in *Who's Afraid of Virginia Woolf?* As the show travelled from Chicago (2010–2011) and Washington, D.C. (2011) to New York City (2012–2013), Letts and co-star Carrie Coon fell in love. The two would have a rather unconventional wedding in the fall of 2013. An emergency gall bladder surgery disrupted their plans for a courthouse wedding, so Coon persuaded the Lutheran minister at Northwestern Memorial Hospital to hold an impromptu service in Letts's recovery room. With Letts in a hospital gown and Coon in leggings and a T-shirt, the two celebrated their nuptials with cranberry juice and challah bread.[14]

Letts drew inspiration for his next play, *Mary Page Marlowe,* from the death of his mother. In 2014 at the age of seventy-six, Billie was diagnosed with leukemia and died from pneumonia a few months later. For Letts, her death raised questions about the nature of identity: "*Mary Page Marlowe* is an internal examination—an examination of identity, of what makes a person a person . . . The death of a parent not only causes you to think a lot about mortality, but your own mortality, which also makes you think about your life's journey."[15] The play, which premiered at Steppenwolf in April 2016, offers eleven scenes from Mary's life at eleven different ages, ranging from ten months to sixty-nine. Performed by six actresses and unfolding non-sequentially, it provides glimpses into her parents' rocky marriage, her college idealism, two divorces, a string of infidelities, the loss of her son to drug abuse, a prison sentence for multiple DUIs, a happy third marriage late in life, and the realization at sixty-nine that she doesn't have long to live. Always strong-willed and independent, Mary wants to be in charge of her own destiny as she struggles against the various pressures that marriage and motherhood place on her identity. Yet these challenges also comment on some of the hierarchies that limit women in America. As she explains to her psychiatrist, "I think that as a woman, a lot of our roles get stipulated for us, and there's only one way to be a wife, be a daughter, be a mom. Be a lover" (36). She recognizes the possible subordination within these roles, and as such, her story is about the impact of gender inequality on a woman's sense of self.

Letts's next two major plays, *The Minutes* and *Linda Vista,* premiered in 2017. *The Minutes,* which became a finalist for the Pulitzer Prize in 2018, is his first overtly political play, but he admits that "all of the plays are somewhat political."[16] The idea of city council meetings intrigued Letts, and he watched hundreds of hours of them on YouTube in preparation for writing the script. As he notes, these meetings, while "unbelievably boring," also reflect "the work of the people. If you get a new street sign on your street it's because somebody had a meeting about it in a town council meeting. So, that was it. That was how I got to a play."[17] Set in the fictional Midwestern town of Big Cherry, this satire of American governance examines the secrets at the heart of regional and national identity. With Shirley Jackson's short story "The Lottery" (1948) and Roman Polanski's *Rosemary's Baby* (1968) as reference points, both of which Letts discussed with the Steppenwolf cast during rehearsals,[18] *The Minutes* shifts from mundane debates over parking and parliamentary procedure to the mysterious fate of former city council member Mr. Carp. The story of his disappearance reveals a deeper secret about the founding myths of the town and of the country itself—myths that belie the truth about the Indigenous bloodshed upon which America was built. Like Johnna's role in *August: Osage County,* the town's complicity in lying about its origins reflects the country's ongoing desire to erase historical truths about white occupation and exploitation. It reflects a failure on the part of America to take responsibility for the past. What emerges in *The Minutes* is a sobering portrait of political power as stemming not from truth but from the power to shape and control historical narrative.

Despite the critical success of *The Minutes,* Letts decided to revise *Linda Vista* first, and Steppenwolf produced it again in 2019 in Los Angeles and New York. The three-hour play, which Letts considers a "favorite," has a scope that rivals *August: Osage County,* and its depiction of Dick Wheeler's midlife crisis offers a meditation on broken families, power, and the legacy of racist ideology in America. After moving out of his ex-wife's garage, Wheeler finds himself in a shabby furnished apartment in Southern California, working as a camera repairman and navigating the dating scene. His mundane job offers a daily reminder of his decision years earlier to abandon photography: "There is enough mediocrity in the world. I didn't need to throw my pictures on the pile." Self-deprecating and opinionated, Wheeler rails against everything from Trump voters to movies made after 1984. His need to affirm his masculinity through sex leads to a string of disastrous relationships. He destroys his newfound romance with Jules, for example, by having an affair with his twenty-six-year-old neighbor, Minnie Tran, and his tendency to view Minnie through the lens of ethnic stereotypes dooms their relationship as well. His biases also comment on the broader tendency in white America to whitewash truths about prejudice. Yet when Wheeler picks up a camera for the first time in years, much like Arthur helping Franco rewrite his novel and Ken attempting sculpture, Letts presents art as a possible tool for breaking down gender and racial hierarchies.

Between 2017 and 2019, Letts's work on *Linda Vista* coincided with his thriving career as an actor and the beginning of his new career as a father. In 2017 alone, he starred in several films including Greta Gerwig's *Lady Bird,* Stephen Spielberg's *The Post,* and the romantic comedy *The Lovers.* His recent television appearances included three seasons of the HBO series *Divorce* (2016–19) and the second season of *The Sinner* (2018) alongside Carrie Coon. The spring of 2019 also marked Letts's return to Broadway with a commanding performance as Joe Keller in the revival of Arthur Miller's *All My Sons.* Amid all of these professional successes, Letts and Coon had their first child, Haskell, in March 2018. For a playwright so interested in family and in characters traumatized by the loss of a child—whether literally like Agnes in *Bug* and

Mary Page Marlowe or figuratively in *Superior Donuts* and *Linda Vista*—it will be interesting to see the ways fatherhood impacts his creative vision. As Letts has said about his own struggles and losses, "There comes a point in your life where you own your own damage. You don't necessarily get over it, you don't necessarily have it all figured out, you just say this is mine, these are things I have to be aware of, take care of, work around."[19] Playwriting has been one of the primary tools for Letts to take care of this damage. He will no doubt continue to mine the personal for social commentary, to challenge cultural biases through humor and wit, and, in one form or another, to ask us to think about our role in shaping the America of tomorrow. As the title of Franco Wicks's novel makes clear, and as Letts's plays remind us again and again, "America Will Be."

Overview

Understanding Tracy Letts celebrates the range of Letts's writing, in part, by applying different critical approaches to his works. In many respects, Letts's oeuvre evokes the kind of genius manifest in writers such as J. M. Coetzee and Vladimir Nabokov. Each of these artists often produced radically different works. At first glance, one might be surprised to discover that Coetzee wrote both *Waiting for the Barbarians* and *Elizabeth Costello* or that Nabokov wrote *Lolita* as well as *Pale Fire*. Likewise, most audiences might be shocked to discover Letts penned both *Killer Joe* and *Man from Nebraska*. Certainly, upon closer examination, we can find thematic and stylistic connections between these plays, but this diversity of craftsmanship and vision demands a diversity of analytical perspectives. A one-size-fits-all approach risks overlooking the nuance and richness of Letts's writing.

The following chapter interprets *Killer Joe* through the lens of the disability theater movement. Letts has noted the influence of Tennessee Williams's *The Glass Menagerie* and William Faulkner's *As I Lay Dying* on his first play, and like *Killer Joe,* these works make disability central to their exploration of poverty. Laura's limp from polio, for example, limits her prospects for marriage in *The Glass Menagerie,* and this has significant financial implications during the Great Depression. Likewise, the cognitive disability of Faulkner's Darl becomes a way to comment on the impact of systemic poverty in the American South. With these models in mind, Letts fashions *Killer Joe* into a portrait of working-poor America as defined by desperation, exploitation, and a callous disregard for others. The Smith family, which is willing to barter Dottie's body for money, represents a country broken by hierarchies that disenfranchise women, the poor, and the disabled. For Letts, Dottie's unspecified disability undercuts the audience's desire to view her metaphorically, and the violence of the play ultimately presents poverty, disability bias, and gender inequity as urgent problems in American culture.

Inspired by the Oklahoma City Bombing in 1995, Letts's second play, *Bug*, explores the intersection of conspiracy culture and poverty in the United States. One of the central characters, Peter, alludes to dozens of government conspiracies from Tuskegee to Oklahoma, but his paranoia would not have surprised most Americans at the time. On a weekly basis, Fox Mulder on *The X-Files*, one of the most popular shows on television, had been espousing Peter's vision of the U.S. government and military since 1993. Together both *Bug* and *The X-Files* capture the way conspiracy ideology shifted from the margins to the center of American life by the end of the twentieth century. They also use the working poor to comment on socioeconomic inequity. Like *Killer Joe*, *Bug* features characters circumscribed by poverty. Agnes White has a dead-end job and a preference for solitude, and she earns just enough money for drugs and alcohol to numb the pain of her son's abduction. Mulder, though financially secure with his white-collar career as an FBI agent, shares a similar anguish over the abduction of his sister. For both characters, conspiracy makes them feel important. It gives their pain a grandeur that matches the depth of their loss. Beginning with a discussion of the conspiracy genre, Chapter Three examines the motif of missing children in *Bug* and *The X-Files* as an image for the forgotten poor and for ignoring the truth about poverty in 1990s America.

Poverty haunts *August: Osage County* as well, and through the critical perspective of food studies and the decolonial food movement, Chapter Four discusses the link between the economic exploitation of Native Americans and food culture. For Letts, food—the contrast between traditional American cuisine and the absence of Native American meals, between vegetarianism and meat eating—captures the legacy of colonialism in the United States. Through wars, broken treaties, stolen land, forced removals, and the reservation system, Native American tribes have been systematically destroyed and marginalized throughout American history. Johnna offers one reminder of this legacy. Her working-poor life as a Cheyenne woman in Oklahoma is emblematic of the social and economic limitations facing many Native Americans. Nevertheless, her deep connection to cultural traditions and family endows her with a strength that the Westons lack. It is Johnna who does the work of family in *August: Osage County*, and her role as a cook exposes the extent of the Westons' dissipation, particularly through their failure to cook or to cook well. While Johnna deftly prepares the food of Americana from fried chicken to apple pie, she never mentions Cheyenne cuisine, and Letts uses the absence of this food to point to the erasure of Indigenous culture more broadly. Furthermore, the Westons' attitude about eating links the exploitation of Native Americans with that of the environment. Whether through Steve's experiences working in the meatpacking industry, Uncle Charlie's need to have meat with every meal, or the family's jokes about vegetarianism, food in the Weston house captures Letts's critique of the various ways white America continues to exploit the land and people of color.

Mary Page Marlowe ends with the titular protagonist asking a dry cleaner about repairing an old quilt. The stained, mostly forgotten artifact features panels of different women in her family dating back to the colonial era. This quilt, an image for the eleven scenes of Mary's life that make up the play, evokes the long tradition of quilting in American culture. Whether as part of girls' education, quilting bees, or decorative arts, the quilt has long served as an outlet for female identity and community. Its role in American life and the arts, including literature, has also been the subject of feminist critics since the 1960s. Chapter Five situates Letts's use of the quilt in this tradition to examine the feminist politics of the play—particularly the role of patriarchy in limiting women's autonomy and selfhood. In many ways, Mary's existential crisis comes from recognizing her shared plight with every other woman in America. The roles of daughter, lover, wife, and mother have been prescribed by patriarchal norms, and as such, they leave her little freedom to discover or express herself as an individual. As she explains to her shrink, "Someone else could have written my diary . . . I *am* unexceptional" (34). Yet breaking with these norms does not bring her happiness. A string of meaningless affairs, for instance, ends her first marriage, and the excessive drinking characterizing her second marriage lands her in jail. These experiences highlight Letts's message about the dangers of social expectations that leave little room for women to find contentment with themselves, with the roles they play, and with others. Like the Marlowe quilt, Letts invites the audience to piece together a portrait of women's lives through Mary. These fragments not only represent the way patriarchy fractures female identity, but they also speak to the desire among women to piece together their own stories, to define motherhood and marriage in ways that do not compromise individual identity.

Chapter Six uses masculinity studies to explore Letts's depiction of aging white men in *Linda Vista, Superior Donuts,* and *Man from Nebraska.* Although the men in these works have largely abandoned the cowboy masculinity of Westerns, they have internalized white patriarchal ideology in ways that continue to impede their happiness. Damaged families—whether the result of divorce or abandonment—become metaphors for the way sexism and racism inhibit the kind of egalitarianism necessary for white male contentment. Dick Wheeler of *Linda Vista,* for example, tends to sexually objectify women and reduce nonwhites to ethnic stereotypes. Arthur Przybyszewski's life in a dingy donut shop embodies his retreat from family, from engaging in social activism, and from the draft, raising questions about his masculinity. And Ken Carpenter's crisis of faith in *Man from Nebraska* makes him recognize his passivity toward life and his need to redefine himself as a man. Letts uses these narratives, particularly the men's relationships with people of color, to challenge white patriarchal modes of thinking. Minnie Tran leaves Wheeler in a way that asserts Vietnamese culture as central to her sense of self. Arthur's decision to care for Franco Wicks and Ken's friendship with Tamyra invite both men to think about the impact of racism on blacks in Western culture. For Letts, these relationships not only confront the problem of white privilege in America, but they also present art as a vehicle for understanding the self and others. Art— whether photography, writing, or sculpture—offers a path for engaging more meaningfully in the world and for defining masculinity through compassionate engagement with others.

As the first book dedicated entirely to his writing, *Understanding Tracy Letts* is both an introduction to his plays and an invitation to engage more deeply with his work—both for how it moves us and for how it comments on America. I have decided to focus on Letts's original works—as opposed to his adaptation of Chekhov's *Three Sisters* and A. J. Finn's novel *The Woman in the Window* (though I discuss the latter in the epilogue)—to keep the spotlight on Letts's innovative vision for American theater. Letts started his career on the stage. He continues to be inspired by and to thrive in that space, and it is where he returns most passionately as a performer, writer, and editor. Though neither of his most recent plays, *Linda Vista* and *The Minutes,* were in print during the writing of this book, I was able to attend several performances of Steppenwolf's 2019 production of *Linda Vista* in Los Angeles, which gave me the opportunity to take detailed notes for its inclusion in Chapter Six. *The Minutes,* however, has yet to be produced again as of this writing, though it is scheduled for a New York premiere in February 2020. For that reason, I am not able to include a detailed discussion of it here. I recognize that no book about Tracy Letts at this stage in his career can be comprehensive. As a young playwright in his early fifties, Letts has many plays still to write, and that is good news for all of us.

CHAPTER 2

Disability and Poverty in *Killer Joe,* *The Glass Menagerie,* and *As I Lay Dying*

In addition to drawing inspiration from "strong, black, very hardcore *noir*,"[1] Tracy Letts based *Killer Joe* on an actual crime committed by a family of drug dealers. The murder, as Letts explains, involved "a mother and son who were going to kill the father . . . [until] the father and son . . . decided to kill her instead [for stealing cocaine]. It was just sort of the ease with which they changed their minds about which family member was going to die, that sparked my thinking about how you gotta get pretty far down when family ties mean so little to you."[2] In many respects, *Killer Joe* is about the forces in American culture—most notably poverty and prejudice—that drag people down. As father-and-son mechanics, Ansel and Chris earn just enough to get by, and Chris pursues one disastrous get-rich-quick scheme after another. Ansel's wife, Sharla, works at Pizza Hut. These economic hardships, like the Smiths' "seedy and cheap" trailer, also function as a metaphor for their moral failings. Chris and Ansel care more about cheating their customers than repairing cars, and they readily exploit Dottie's disability. Killer Joe takes sadistic pleasure in denigrating Sharla and Dottie. And no one hesitates at the idea of murder for profit. Poverty and prejudice, in other words, trap these characters, reducing women to sexual objects, denigrating the disabled, and relegating a person's value to the dollar amount on an insurance policy.

Killer Joe begins with Chris, Ansel, and Sharla's decision to hire a hitman to kill Chris's biological mother, Adele. Chris wants the settlement from her life insurance policy to pay off a dangerous drug dealer, whereas Ansel and Sharla merely like the idea of having money (though for different reasons).

Since the family cannot pay Detective "Killer" Joe Cooper upfront, they offer him Chris's cognitively disabled sister, Dottie, as a "retainer." Her sexual exploitation becomes a disturbing image for the extent to which these characters use each other. The narrative culminates with the revelation that Rex, Sharla's secret lover and Adele's boyfriend, manipulated Chris into the crime. Rex is the actual beneficiary of the policy and its double indemnity clause, but his windfall proves short-lived when Joe learns of the deception. In short, everyone gets double-crossed in *Killer Joe*. Just as Sharla operates as a type of femme fatale, assuming that her affair with Rex will benefit her, Dottie becomes the literal embodiment of this archetype.[3] She shoots Chris and Ansel in the closing moments. And even though Joe has convinced himself that they are "in love," the play ends ambiguously when she announces her pregnancy and points a gun at him with "her finger tensed on the trigger" (82).

The economic narrative of the Smith family underscores *Killer Joe's* broader exploration of American poverty. The play, which premiered at the Next Theatre Lab on August 3, 1993, was mostly conceived during the recession of 1990 to 1991. This downturn stemmed in part from the 1989 Savings and Loan Crisis and the spike in gasoline prices caused by the Gulf War (August 2, 1990, to February 28, 1991). Likewise, as Colin Harrison explains, "rising levels of employment occurred simultaneously with the business practice known as 'downsizing,' which saw over sixteen million Americans dismissed from their jobs in the period 1992–1998 (roughly amounting to one in every fourteen working adults); many of these were forced to take a lower-wage job in returning to work" (7). No news about these issues blares through the massive television in the Smiths' trailer. Instead, the family watches only escapist fodder such as monster truck rallies, karate movies, game shows, cartoons, and police procedurals, capturing the way popular culture discourages engagement with political and social matters. Although money only partially explains their plan to kill Adele, Letts makes poverty—and the desperation it inspires—a crisis that demands attention.

At the same time, Dottie's character puts *Killer Joe* in dialogue with two of the most famous twentieth-century American works about poverty and disability, *The Glass Menagerie* (1944) and *As I Lay Dying* (1930). Letts himself has described *Killer Joe* as "[echoing] the influence of Faulkner and Tennessee Williams," and his work on this manuscript coincided with his appearance in a production of *The Glass Menagerie* at the time.[4] All of these works share a similar preoccupation with economic deprivation.[5] *The Glass Menagerie* portrays tenement life during the Great Depression as characterized by a perpetual anxiety about money. The Wingfield family buys food on credit and struggles to pay the bills. Laura's failure to learn typing causes her mother, Amanda, to lament: "What is there left but dependency all our lives?" (16). And Tom maintains a stultifying job at Continental Shoemakers to provide for his mother and sister. In discussing the importance of the play's social commentary, Christopher Bigsby notes that Tom's "decision to leave has financial as well as personal implications. He earns a wretched sixty-five dollars a month but in Depression America any job is valuable" ("Entering," 34). Likewise, Faulkner's *As I Lay Dying,* which he began writing feverishly the day after the market crash on October 24, 1929,[6] captures the economic hardships of rural life in the South. The Bundren family lives in abject poverty. The father, Anse, steals money from his children, relies on charity from his neighbors, and refuses to solicit medical help for ailing family members because of the expense. For Faulkner, the Bundren's lives comment on the realities of poverty at the outset of the Depression. As historian David Kyvig argues, "Even at the end of the economic surge of the 1920s, poverty was the usual situation for at least two-fifths of the American population . . . The poor labored to pay for food and shelter, rarely could afford to buy clothing much less new consumer goods, and certainly did not participate in the stock market boom. The 1930s depression would intensify their struggle but otherwise represent nothing new in terms of their daily lives" (211).

On another level, these works place disability at the center of working-poor life. In *The Glass Menagerie,* Laura's limp from a bout with polio earns her the label "crippled," and her history of medical problems, along with her shyness, is viewed as a sign of fragility. Yet Williams undercuts these interpretations through behaviors that make her like everyone else—such as romanticizing the past, longing for love, listening to records, going to art museums, and visiting the zoo. Many of Faulkner's characters in *As I Lay Dying* suffer from physical disabilities as well. Anse has been without teeth for fifteen years. Cash violently breaks his leg twice, and Peabody's fatness inhibits his mobility. More significant, Darl has some type of cognitive impairment, inspiring most of the characters to label him "queer," and this condition plays a crucial role in the novel's depiction of disability. His insights into human nature, which escape the rest of the family, cast disability as enabling, not limiting. Darl thus becomes a vehicle for Faulkner to blur the line between normal and abnormal and to raise questions about the way society stigmatizes difference.

In *Killer Joe,* Dottie Smith emerges as a fusion of both Laura and Darl with one crucial difference. Dottie asserts her power by refusing to let the Smith family circumscribe her. Like Laura and Darl, Dottie is perceived as different: "That girl's not like other people, goddam it" (32). Yet she proves more astute—and dangerous—than the rest of her family, showing herself capable in ways that no one acknowledges or recognizes. While all of these works reveal poverty to be socially and morally damaging, they do not use the disabled body as a metaphor for economic hardship. They present physical and mental disabilities in their own terms to challenge prejudice. After beginning with an overview of disability activism and its intersection with the performing arts, this chapter analyzes the role of disability in *The Glass Menagerie* and *As I Lay Dying*, arguing that Letts reworks these classic texts in ways that resonate with the politics of the disability theater movement. Dottie's character confronts audiences with their own misconceptions about the disabled, and her role in the play suggests an urgent need to correct these problems. Finally, a brief discussion of the 2018 London revival of *Killer Joe* highlights the lingering challenges of representing disability today and of confronting social biases that continue to limit the disabled.

Activism, Disability Studies, and the Theater

As many scholars have noted, disability activism emerged, in part, as a response to the ways scientific discourse viewed the extraordinary body in terms of cure, prevention, and rehabilitation. This perspective in Western culture can be traced to the shift from viewing the anomalous body as a sign of divine will in the ancient world to a "freak of nature" in the post-Enlightenment era— something scientists would categorize as teratology, or the study of monsters, by 1832.[7] For Michael Davidson, this medicalized model served the dominant power structure by imposing meaning on these bodies to "assist [the] productive apparatus of capitalism" (18). Examples of this range from nineteenth-century freak shows to modern buildings without wheelchair access.

Activists ultimately responded to this tradition of scientific and marketplace narratives through two models: the social construction model and the minority model. In 1975 the Union of Physically Impaired Against Segregation (UPIAS) established the foundation for the social construction model by defining disability as "the disadvantage or restriction of activity caused by a contemporary social organization which takes little or no account of people who have physical impairments and thus excludes them from participation in the mainstream of social activities."[8] This definition recognizes that society— as evidenced by the majority of sidewalks, buildings, and modes of public transportation—has been designed predominantly for the nondisabled. According to Tom Shakespeare, the social construction model makes an important distinction between impairment and disability: "The former is individual and private, the latter is structural and public" (197). It also views the disabled as "an oppressed group," recognizing that "often non-disabled people and organizations—such as professionals and charities—are the causes or contributors to that oppression" (198). This model has helped build a powerful community committed to identifying these types of social barriers and to improving the self-image of those with disabilities.

The minority model focuses on issues of exclusion and marginality as well. According to Carrie Sandahl and Philip Auslander, it considers the disabled "a distinct minority community that has been . . . [denied] full participation in society because of discrimination in education, employment, and architectural access" (8). This approach aligns the experiences of the disabled with other marginalized groups such as African Americans, women, and LGBTQ people. As such, the minority model insists on recognizing the body as a vehicle for diversity. This approach has helped forge a broader constituency for political activism, and it unites the efforts of the minority model with the social construction model by asserting that social forces (in this case prejudice), not biology, oppress the disabled.

Both models have played a critical role in the legislative accomplishments of disability rights activism. The Architectural Barriers Act of 1968, for example, mandated accessibility to public places and transportation. A few years later, Section 504 of the Rehabilitation Act of 1973 provided the disabled with equal access to federally funded programs, making it "the first civil rights act extending protection to such persons."[9] The Education of All Handicapped Children Act of 1975 (renamed the Individuals with Disabilities Education Act or IDEA in 1990) protected children from discrimination in public schools, insisting on equal access and "one free meal a day for all children with physical or mental disabilities" (Kochhar-Lindgren 81). These efforts culminated in the Americans with Disabilities Act of 1990—a comprehensive law designed to protect the disabled from discrimination in employment, public services, transportation, and education. It also required employers to provide "reasonable accommodation" and access. Overall, as historians Paul K. Longmore and Lauri Umanski have noted, the fifty Congressional acts addressing people with disabilities between 1968 and 1990 reflected a new perspective and definition of disability that developed from "the campaigning of disabled people and their nondisabled allies" (10).

Contributing to and inspired by these efforts, academia and the arts have approached disability as a social and cultural phenomenon. The first wave of disability studies emerged in the fields of sociology and political science with the goal of "providing an analytical research base for the reform of public policies and professional practices" (Longmore and Umanski 12). This wave, which occurred in the 1980s, tended to be skeptical about representations of disability in the arts, viewing these works as perpetuating stereotypes. As Lennard J. Davis explains, many literary works often "have some reference to the abnormal . . . [to create and bolster] images of normalcy" (10). In the 1990s, however, the second wave of disability studies—this time emerging within the humanities—sought to examine these types of representations. It addressed, and attempted to redress, the social limitations imposed on the disabled, and its focus on social practices, public policy, and artistic portrayals urged a richer understanding of the way the body is constructed and interpreted.

These efforts coincided with the rise of the disability arts movement. For Kirsty Johnston, an important link exists between art and disability activism: "By claiming a place for disability experience in the arts as worthy and valuably different, the movement took aim at hackneyed stereotypes and the recurring use of disabilities as metaphors for something else" (21). She places theater at the center of these efforts, praising dramatic works that critique the tendency either to use clichéd portrayals of disability or to render it invisible. These artist–activists also protest hiring nondisabled actors to play disabled characters, and they encourage work about the disabled experience. "As part of the larger disability arts and culture movement, disability theatre is broadly connected to impulses for social justice in the face of ableist ideologies and practices as well as a profound recognition of disabled lives and experiences as inherently valuable" (25). Sandahl and Auslander have noted the similar goals of disability studies and performance studies, which share "academic–activist roots, interdisciplinarity, the body as primary object of study, an international scope, and an interest in the politics and dynamics of representation" (5). In their introduction to *Bodies in Commotion: Disability and Performance,* they insist that legislative strides in disability rights "would not have been possible without activists', artists', and scholars' insistence on new ways of considering disability" (8). Victoria Ann Lewis likewise emphasizes the importance of disabled playwrights, and her groundbreaking anthology *Beyond Victims and Villains: Contemporary Plays by Disabled Playwrights* argues "for the centrality of disability to our understanding of social and collective life, not because the disabled person instructs us about individual acts of courage in the face of tragic loss, but rather because the impaired body makes manifest the impossibility of living life without community" (xliv).

Though the authors examined in this chapter have never been labeled disabled (excluding the time Faulkner fabricated a war injury after Armistice), their depiction of disability embraces some of the goals of disability activism. In the case of Letts's *Killer Joe* and Williams's *The Glass Menagerie,* disability gets presented in ways that challenge the audience's tendency to view difference as a personal limitation either to hide or to "fix" in some way. Faulkner's *As I Lay Dying* contains a similar message about normalcy and deviance. Darl's madness—like Dottie's rage and Laura's silence—is a response to socially constructed views of disability as something shameful. Together, these works present prejudices about the extraordinary body as a problem that demands social as well as ideological change.

Dressing Up: Disability and Gentlemen Callers in *The Glass Menagerie*

The portrait of disability in Tennessee Williams's *The Glass Menagerie,* which premiered at Chicago's Civic Theatre on December 26, 1944,[10] has typically been viewed through a biographical lens. In brief, Williams based Laura Wingfield on his sister, Rose, who was institutionalized in a state hospital for schizophrenia in 1937. As biographer Lyle Leverich notes, this disorder at the time "yielded little to analysis or to the medical treatments of either insulin shock or Metrazol therapy but . . . devastated one's ability in the areas of thinking, concentration, memory, and perception" (481). In January 1943, hospital doctors tried a more invasive approach and performed a prefrontal lobotomy on Rose. Many scholars have viewed this play as an expression of Williams's "attempt to come to terms with his sister's illness and perhaps exorcize his guilt over not having taken more measures in trying to prevent the operation" (Bray viii). Regardless of his intentions, Williams's depiction of Laura has been a source of contention among disability scholars. Deborah Kent, for instance, has discussed the troubling theatrical tradition of presenting disabled women as self-pitying, undesirable, helpless, and economically dependent: "Whether she is blind or deaf, facially disfigured or paraplegic, the disabled woman is typically shown to be incomplete not only in body, but in the basic expression of her womanhood" (93). For Kent, Laura takes on the "saintly" stereotype—a woman who "has assumed the world's view of her as asexual, dependent, a perennial child" (96). This failing of *The Glass Menagerie* comes, in part, from the fact that "for most spectators, the play evokes no sense of outrage against the forces that have kept Laura from living fully. It is the image of the poor crippled girl—forever a child playing with her glass animals—that lingers on" (98).

Scholar Ann M. Fox echoes this frustration with the play's message about the body: "Disability, as it has appeared onstage in American drama in characters such as Laura Wingfield, has amounted to a sort of gentrified freak show, allowing audiences the opportunity to look at disabled bodies metaphorically and voyeuristically . . . When audience members define these social constructions of disability as normal, their collective stare restages what happens outside the theater walls in everyday life" ("But Mother," 234). Over ten years later, however, Fox revisited her reading of *The Glass Menagerie* and found the play's disability politics more subversive than she had originally recognized. She specifically praises the play's tendency to find the "ordinary in the seeming extraordinary . . . It is not so much that Laura's disability makes her more special; it is that the world's masking of her variation reflects a larger tendency for it to willfully forget its own varied self" ("Reclaiming," 141). Williams's condemnation of this cultural push for uniformity works in tandem with his presentation of Laura's average qualities. In many ways, Laura proves to be like everyone else around her. As Fox explains, "I think, ironically, to see what makes Laura special, potentially even radical as a disabled character, we have to see how common she is; and by 'common,' I do not mean 'conformist.' There is something decidedly ordinary about Laura" (141). The prosaic nature of her desires, in other words, undercuts attempts at viewing her body as a spectacle. It invites audiences to think about the harm caused by stigmatizing difference and by excluding a disability perspective in American culture.

More specifically, Williams uses Laura's shyness and glass unicorn to critique social mores that demand a kind of erasure of the disabled body. Laura remembers wearing a leg brace in high school that "clumped so loud . . . it sounded like thunder!" (75), and these feelings of embarrassment, which led her to drop out of school, stem from the way "people outside the house" view her as "peculiar" (48). She has learned to equate disability with exclusion, claiming she cannot have a career or get married because she is "crippled" (17). As Fox explains, "Laura's shyness is not simply an innate quality; rather it is tied directly to how she has been made conscious of her physical and emotional difference" (137). Laura's unicorn functions in a similar way. She tells Jim, the gentleman caller, that her unicorn "stays on the shelf with some horses that don't have horns and all of them seem to get along nicely together" (83). In 1930s America, however, glass animals seem to be the only ones capable of forming a community that accepts bodily variation. Only when Laura articulates a narrative about being like everyone else does Jim find her difference from other girls attractive. She even describes her broken unicorn as medically altered to accommodate his discomfort: "I'll just imagine he had an operation. The horn was removed to make him feel less—freakish! Now he will feel more at home with other horses, the ones that don't have horns" (86). Laura recognizes that earning Jim's affection requires her to label disability as freakish and to validate the importance he places on belonging. Jim is, after all, someone who lauds the virtues of appearance, most notably through public speaking, and he proclaims a gift for recognizing the faults in others ("I can sure guess a person's psychology, Laura!" [81]). To some extent, this exchange about the unicorn hints at her fate in American society. She will need to sacrifice her distinctiveness to live the kind of life Jim—and arguably most gentlemen callers—could offer her.

Williams continues this critique through Amanda's desire to rid her family of abnormality. She struggles with having such *"unusual* children" (31) and even pleads with them to change: "Why can't you and your brother be normal people? Fantastic whims and behavior!" (57). For Amanda, imaginative impulses and shyness threaten social norms that provide economic stability. Tom, for example, hides in darkened movie theaters and endangers his job by withdrawing from his coworkers to write poetry. Laura abandons typing classes to listen to old records, tend glass animals, and go to the zoo. Although Amanda fails to alter these predilections, she desperately tries to render Laura's disability invisible. She begins by forbidding her children from using the term "crippled": "Why, you're not crippled, you just have a little defect—hardly noticeable, even! When people have some slight disadvantage like that, they cultivate other things to make up for it—develop charm—and vivacity—and *charm!* That's all you have to do!" (17–18). This philosophy links disability with defects and disadvantages to overcome. As Kent has argued, Amanda considers her daughter's condition unspeakable, "something that must be denied and hidden away. To be 'crippled' is somehow shameful, a disgrace. Laura has never been allowed to acknowledge her lameness as a part of herself" (97). At the same time, Amanda's insistence on masking disability through "charm" reveals her understanding of society's investment in surfaces. Everything in the play suggests that Laura will need to "pass" as able-bodied in order to find either work or a husband—her only paths to economic security.

For Williams, Tom and Jim also engage in the harmful practice of using the disabled body to assert normalcy. To some degree, Tom recognizes the way external forces shape the perception of disability: "We don't even notice she's crippled any more . . . Laura is different from other girls . . . In the eyes of others—strangers—she's terribly shy and lives in a world of her own and those things make her seem peculiar to people outside of the house" (47–8). Tom blames society for being hostile to difference, yet he erases Laura's body from this assessment. Terrible shyness, a preoccupation with glass ornaments, and playing "old phonograph records" cripple Laura, not her limp. Immediately after this description, Tom catches his reflection in the mirror, and this detail suggests that he is just another version of Laura. Substitute records for movies and glass animals for poetry, and Tom proves no different, no less "crippled," than his sister. Unable to accept such a possibility, Tom contrasts Laura's interior life with his own. He, in effect, uses her "peculiar" habits to normalize himself. Williams underscores this double standard with Tom's closing, guilt-ridden monologue, which renders Laura a tableau. Neither he nor the audience get her interpretation of Jim's visit, so Tom's monologue reduces her to a silent spectacle—someone whose body and supposed grief remain on display. Williams does grant Laura some power here, however. When she blows out the candle, she ends the play by cutting off access to her and her story. The darkness that follows suggests the limits of the audience's (and Tom's) understanding of her. It becomes a reminder of the inherent folly in trying to understand disability without the perspective of those experiencing it.

Jim proves no different when he lectures Laura on disability as a state of mind: "You know what I judge to be the trouble with you? Inferiority complex! . . . A little physical defect is what you have . . . Think of yourself as *superior* in some way!" (81). On one level, as Fox argues, "the play mocks medical paternalism through Jim's diagnostic pretentions" (139). On another level, this moment highlights the contradiction between individualism and homogeneity at the heart of American culture. Jim praises Laura for being different "because other people are not such wonderful people . . . They walk all over the earth. You just stay here" (87). Yet he proves to be just like the not-so-wonderful masses. He kisses Laura only to reveal his engagement to another woman. He hopes to achieve distinction through mass-marketed courses on public speaking and radio engineering. And he finds additional validation for his upwardly mobile aspirations by contrasting them with Laura's sedentary life. Even his term for *faux pas*, "Stumblejohn," underscores his clumsy investment in movement. Jim prefers a state of perpetual motion, changing interests, switching careers, and redefining himself at will, for he considers versatility essential to national and personal progress: "Full steam . . . *Knowledge*—Zzzzzp! *Money* —Zzzzzp!—*Power!* That's the cycle democracy is built on!" (82). Disability, however, remains a fixed identity in the play. Laura does not stay home by choice but for fear of embarrassment and ridicule. She does not have Jim's (or Tom's) access—being neither able-bodied nor male—to experiment freely with new identities and mobility. In these ways, Williams highlights the failures within American culture to accommodate difference. It has denied her any sense of equal opportunity and freedom because of her body and gender.

Finally, Williams uses Laura's sexuality to challenge disability bias as well. Laura pines for a high school boy named Jim O'Connor, and her lengthy encounter with him in Scene Seven, which includes dancing and a kiss, depicts her own sexual longings (79). These details universalize her experiences; in fact, they make Laura more common than Tom in his brooding isolation. Yet when Amanda dresses Laura to make her feel like every other young woman being courted, she equates disability with undesirability. Laura's stillness in this dressing scene, with her arms in the air as her mother adjusts the hem, may hide her physical disability for the moment, but the play has offered repeated reminders of Laura's very real bodily challenges. She stumbles and falls. She has a history of respiratory problems, and she vomits in typing class from nervousness. This contrast explains Williams's description of her beauty as ephemeral. It is a *"momentary radiance, not actual, not lasting"* (51) because this act of standing still masks various truths about her body. Amanda stuffs powder puffs in Laura's bosom, for instance, because her "chest is flat," and she argues that "all pretty girls are a trap, a pretty trap" (52). For Amanda, the messiness of real bodies ought to be hidden, and this gives Laura no real chance to accept herself, no chance to view her body as sexual. For Williams, however, making the audience acutely aware of her disability alongside her *"unearthly prettiness"* forces them to see the disabled body as beautiful (51). It gives them a perspective that society and family have denied Laura.

Disability in William Faulkner's *As I Lay Dying*

In a sudden outburst of creativity, William Faulkner began *As I Lay Dying* the day after Black Thursday in 1929. He worked the nightshift in a powerhouse at the time, and this job gave him ample opportunity to write. As he explained later, the boiler did not require much coal to make steam between 11 PM and 4 AM, so he could dedicate that time to writing—each word accompanied by the constant humming of the dynamo through the wall.[11] Six weeks later he completed the novel. Like *Killer Joe,* Faulkner's text is about the death of a matriarch, but instead of plotting her murder, the Bundrens undertake a perilous forty-mile journey to bury Addie Bundren with her kin in Jefferson, Mississippi. Addie's children—Cash, Darl, Jewell, Dewey Dell, and Vardaman—struggle to cope with the loss of their mother alongside the harsh economic conditions of the rural South. Throughout the text, the Bundrens often view one another in terms of economic utility. Jewell's secret night job, for example, needs to be offset by the labor of his siblings, and Cash's broken leg, which happens while working for someone else, prevents him from making repairs at home. Disability also plays a role in this calculus, for Darl's cognitive impairment proves too costly for the family socially and financially.

Letts announces the influence of Faulkner on *Killer Joe* through an epigraph from *As I Lay Dying:* "How often have I lain beneath rain on a strange roof, thinking of home?" This line comes from Darl, the character considered most unusual by others. He has the reputation for being "the one folks talks about" (64), for "[thinking] by himself too much" (41), for lacking intelligence ("the one that aint bright" [88]), and for laughing inexplicably: "Darl begun to laugh . . . How many times I told him it's doing such things as that that makes folks talk about him" (61). He speaks with a disconcerting monotone, "like he never give a durn himself one way or the other" (110), and people label him "different" and "queer" on numerous occasions. Much of this "queerness" is the result of his stare. His sister, Dewey Dell, compares it to undressing her (69), and one neighbor describes it as extrasensory: "He dont say nothing; just looks at me with them queer eyes of hisn that makes folks talk. I always say it aint never been what he done so much or said or anything so much as how he looks at you. It's like he had got into the inside of you, someway. Like somehow you was looking at yourself and your doings outen his eyes" (72).

Darl's clairvoyance does not bring him closer to his family, however. His insights only isolate him further by making those around him feel resentful and violated. Jewell becomes enraged by Darl's suggestions that Addie is not his biological mother, and his knowledge of Dewey Dell's pregnancy fills her with hate. Ultimately, the Bundrens institutionalize Darl after he burns down a barn to destroy the rotting corpse of his mother. The family does so, in part, for financial reasons, hoping his mental illness will enable them to sidestep any legal responsibility for the barn. At the same time, this moment is decidedly personal. Dewey Dell jumps on her brother, "scratching and clawing at him like a wild cat"; Anse and Jewell "throwed Darl down and held him," while Jewell yells, "Kill him. Kill the son of a bitch" (137). Even though Cash comes across as the most sympathetic of the family, his sensibility as a carpenter trumps kinship, for he cannot forgive the intentional destruction of property, "of what a man has built with his own sweat" (137). He concludes that incarceration is in Darl's best interest.

The Bundrens set on Darl like pack of wild animals—much like the Smiths' treatment of Chris in the closing moments of *Killer Joe*—and Faulkner suggests that part of this anger stems from a desire to rid the family of disability. As Anse explains to Darl at one point, "I got some regard for what folks says about my flesh and blood even if you haven't" (61), and Faulkner uses such details to highlight some of the social forces that stigmatize the disabled. This may help explain why Faulkner obscures the exact nature of Darl's impairment. Unlike Cash's broken legs, Anse's missing teeth, and arguably Peabody's fatness, Darl has no physical disability, nor does he demonstrate the extreme cognitive limitations of Benjy Compson in *The Sound and the Fury* (1929). Darl's perspective begins the novel, and this role as a seemingly objective narrator establishes Darl's individuality *before* there is any implication of disability. Likewise, Faulkner presents him alongside the rest of the Bundrens whose disturbing behaviors—such as Jewell's rage, Anse's selfishness, and Cash's calculating nature—defy norms. Faulkner even questions the labels of "sanity" and "insanity" explicitly through Cash's observations: "I aint so sho that ere a man has the right to say what is crazy and what aint. It's like there was a fellow in every man . . . that watches the sane and insane doings of that man with the same horror and the same astonishment" (137). By putting Darl's actions in this familial and social context, Faulkner blurs the line between normal and abnormal, able and disabled.

Not surprisingly, critics have struggled to label Darl, though most have settled on the general term of "madness." Eric Sundquist examines the character's perceptivity in this way: "Unable to contain his consciousness within the boundaries of sanity, Darl expresses his madness through hallucination and clairvoyance" (34–5). David Kleinbard argues that the novel maps Darl's gradually developing schizophrenia, and several scholars have identified shell shock as another possible source, citing Darl's "time in France at the war" (146). More recently, Taylor Hagood's *Faulkner, Writer of Disability* describes Darl as "psychosocially disabled," for he fails to fit into town norms that the Bundrens desire (126). Hagood's term seems particularly apt in highlighting both the personal harm of being a Bundren and the social context for viewing disability as a source of shame, as something to be rendered invisible.

Whatever trauma Darl experienced as a soldier goes unremarked in the novel; rather, he comes across as more scarred by family life—particularly from a lack of parental affection and general sense of alienation among his siblings and the community. His wanderlust, which Anse describes as having "eyes full of the land" (22), has been replaced by the economic entrapment of rural Southern life and of being a Bundren. Hagood further argues that "the family members eject Darl from their midst because he is a false limb that is no longer needed because they see him as being unable to attain normal status. They now have teeth, bananas, a graphophone, a new mother/wife, all items representative of the cultural center that is town, even if they are not themselves living in that center. All of these things are prosthetics that the Bundrens substitute for Darl and/or Addie" (121). In other words, the Bundrens' upwardly mobile aspirations—namely the desire to find acceptance within town culture and to acquire goods to mitigate the debilitating impact of poverty on their lives—make disability too great a liability to bear.

Killer Dottie: Disability in 1990s America

Letts's *Killer Joe* can be viewed through the lens of the disability arts movement, in part, because it rejects the theatrical and literary tradition of reading disability as metaphor—what David T. Mitchell and Sharon L. Snyder refer to as "narrative prosthesis," using disability as "a symbolic vehicle for meaning-making and cultural critique" (1). For Mitchell and Snyder, this tendency attempts to control or normalize a body that appears deviant, for it presents disability as something that "derives value from its noncompliance with social expectations about valid physical and cognitive lives" (9). *Killer Joe*, by contrast, establishes an ambiguity about Dottie's impairment and potential for violence to undermine the audience's desire to label and interpret her as a victim. For Letts, reductionist labels foster exploitation, as the sexual violence against Dottie illustrates, yet her assertion of power at the end of the play demands an understanding of her that transcends the body.

Letts's ambiguous portrait of Dottie offers one example of the play's resistance to viewing her primarily through the lens of disability. Unlike Laura's limp in *The Glass Menagerie,* no physical disability is ascribed to Dottie. Instead, she is introduced to the audience with a hazy uncertainty. She first appears "sleep talkin'," and her opening dialogue with Chris and Ansel establishes a destabilizing complexity about her character. She asks if Chris "built this city," explaining that she "heard that at a wedding," and when Ansel dismisses her talk as sleep-walking gibberish, Dottie replies, "I'm not asleep, I'm just workin'" (17). Throughout the play, Dottie vacillates between abstraction and pointed commentary—much like Faulkner's Darl—in ways that make it difficult to assess her character. She lives in a world of imagination and gets lost in the blaring banality of modern American television—practicing martial arts while watching karate movies and pondering the coyote's fate in *The Road Runner* cartoons. Letts contrasts this escapist dimension of television with Dottie's insight and directness. She gives her approval for "killin' Momma" the moment the plan is hatched (18). She jokes about poison after Joe takes a bite of casserole (40). She knows of Sharla's affair (30), and she understands that the plan for the insurance money has fallen apart: "They're not gonna pay you the money, are they?" (57). In fact, such incisiveness forces the audience to question the family's assessment of Dottie. The Smiths generally dismiss her abilities, both cognitive and physical, and this encourages the audience to do so as well. Yet Dottie offers her own disability narrative, claiming that she remembers the time "momma tried to kill me when I was real little. She put a pillow over my face and tried to stop me from breathing . . . She only made me sick, made me not be for a while; but then I was and she was sad" (23). This language is deceptive, however. Dottie defines sickness as nearly dying ("made me not be"), not as cognitive impairment, and Killer Joe doubts her ability to remember the incident. Once again, Letts uses this indeterminacy to prevent the audience from defining Dottie solely by her disability.

Her comments about Chris, which initially seem unclear but prove trenchant, also serve to undercut a metaphorical reading of her character. Her initial question to Chris about building the city, for example, has to do with personal responsibility. Chris responds that he built it "brick by brick," and the audience soon recognizes Chris as the architect of his own demise, always looking for a quick-fix solution to his problems. When Dottie later watches *The Road Runner* "to see how it turned out," Chris dismissively responds: "He doesn't catch the bird, okay?! It just goes on and on and on!" (55). Yet he fails to recognize the connection between himself and the coyote—an opportunistic scavenger that perpetually seeks a prize forever out of reach. Dottie's insightfulness makes it difficult for the audience to pinpoint the exact nature of her difference, and these moments undercut the Smiths' interpretation of disability as a liability. This ambiguity thus enables Letts to challenge the way society uses disability to define, dismiss, marginalize, and undervalue the disabled. Without providing a label for her behavior, the play forces the audience to consider and evaluate Dottie on her own terms. It forces the audience to question its need to find a label for Dottie and for difference more broadly.

Letts also reworks two important details from *The Glass Menagerie*— Laura's childhood crush and her evening gown—to establish a link between the threat of sexual exploitation and disability bias. Early in the play, Dottie recalls a romantic fantasy from her youth: "I had a boyfriend in the third grade, but I never told nobody. His name was Marshall and he was fat" (30). Marshall's fatness, like Jim's freckled skin,[12] highlights the way bodily ideals tend to determine a person's value in America. Her affinity for Marshall stems, in part, from the way fatness marginalizes him, so she views this romance as transcending the physical. She kept it secret, explaining that she and Marshall never saw each other outside of school or spoke about their feelings. Sharla interprets this story as a sign both of Dottie's innocence ("she's never even been on a real date before") and of her developmental limitations. Yet this fantasy reveals Dottie's longing to escape the social stigmas associated with difference—whether fatness or disability. It also reflects an ongoing struggle to reconcile her history of sexual abuse with the depiction of love on television. Later in the play, she recalls an incident in which Chris "just . . . laid on top of me. He stretched his body out, like this, and laid on me, until I stopped cryin'" (41). Moments later Joe commands her to touch his penis, and she compares the experience to being twelve years old (43). Together, these details suggest that Chris raped her at that age. This assault taught Dottie to disassociate love from sex. Not surprisingly, she harkens back to a nine-year-old romance—an age before her rape and before the complexities of sexuality—to define love. Her sexual assault, however, gets subsumed by the disability bias within the Smith family. Since they perceive Dottie as disabled, her trauma can be attributed to impairment, abdicating any personal responsibility for their actions. They can, in other words, use disability to continue to objectify and abuse her. The intersection of these narratives (of the sexualized body and the disabled body) enables Letts to critique patriarchal oppression by connecting it with a social ideology that denigrates the disabled. Both foster exploitation and injustice. And both get connected with violence to suggest the urgency of correcting such attitudes.

The preparations for Dottie's gentleman caller offer another example of this link between the exploitation of female sexuality and disability. When Joe first comes to dinner, Ansel insists that Dottie dress provocatively, and he even asks her to stand on a chair to inspect her "sexy black" gown: "You look like a goddamn movie star" (33). Ansel does not alter Dottie's outfit—the way Amanda Wingfield modifies Laura's dress through sewing and powder puffs—but he does want Dottie to appear sexually enticing for Joe, hoping her physical beauty will compensate for any perceived limitation and convince Joe to murder his ex-wife. During this dressing scene, Ansel compliments his daughter's beauty, yet his reference to movies proves double-edged. Dottie's world revolves around television shows, film, and fashion magazines. She even fantasizes about going to "modelin' school" and looking like "Christie Brinkley" (56). These details indicate the extent to which she assesses her own body by such standards.[13] Not surprisingly, Dottie complains that her "butt's too big" (34), and she rejects Ansel's assertion that many men find this quality attractive. Body fat of any kind deviates from the norms of Hollywood and magazines, and these sources have taught Dottie not to view herself as beautiful. Even her attitude toward Marshall's fatness never translates into an acceptance of her own body. She simply cannot escape the way men objectify her. Not surprisingly, when Ansel proceeds to fondle her butt while she stands on the chair, she does not react with shock. Instead, she continues their conversation without hesitation or reproach, suggesting that she is accustomed to such treatment. Disability once again becomes a justification to abuse Dottie. For Letts, it also highlights the dangers of a culture that places so much value on the body and promotes bodily ideals that ensure the devaluation of those who fail to achieve or maintain them.

Only when she discovers that Joe plans to dine with her privately does she protest, and after Ansel grabs her, her reaction suggests the need to shift social as well as individual perceptions about disability. As Dottie pleads, "I have to change, I have to change . . . I HAVE TO CHANGE" (34–5). Literally, Dottie plans to change out of the clothes that make her feel exposed, "funny," and "not me" (34, 41). She recognizes that the dress functions as an invitation for male exploitation. It causes Ansel to grope her, and after Joe commands her to wear the dress, he orders her to touch his penis. Her insistence on changing thus suggests a desire not to be read either as a sexual object (she puts on jeans and a sweatshirt instead) or as disabled. Dottie resists such interpretations ("It's not me") because these perceptions of women and the disabled deny individuality. As a sexual object and as someone with a perceived disability, she recognizes that other people feel justified using her. Ansel even concludes that giving her to Joe "might just do her some good" (27), and Joe subsequently describes her with the pronoun "it": "It belongs to me. And I'm taking it with me when I leave" (73). From the likely rape by her brother and Ansel's harassment to her sexual encounters with Joe, Dottie is part of a familial and social culture that makes her an object of abuse.

At the same time, Letts uses Dottie's violence to reject any clichéd link between disability and victimhood. Dottie hints at her own potential for violence throughout the play, warning Chris at one point about her temper (62). Her brother and father hire a hitman, for example, because they cannot bring themselves to kill Mrs. Smith, but Dottie shows no such hesitation. Perhaps it is not surprising that she shoots Chris and Ansel when the kitchen becomes a battleground. With Ansel, Sharla, and Joe yelling "kill him" and "die" as they try to beat him to death in the refrigerator, Dottie can no longer tolerate it (81). The kitchen has been the only space in the trailer that maintains the illusion of family. It is where they go (for beer), and it is where she cooks and feeds them. In fact, Dottie appears to be the only one who cooks, making a tuna casserole and coffee, and she even offers to prepare a salad "if people're hungry enough" (29). Although it is difficult to imagine anyone in the Smith family eating salad or anything else nutritious, Dottie mixes ingredients to make something of substance, and she willingly dresses up for a family meal, suggesting the value of shared food and company.

Of course, no one in the family eats together until Killer Joe forces them with the threat of violence. This dining scene becomes a parody of the family dinner as typified by Norman Rockwell's Thanksgiving painting *Freedom from Want* (1943). The Smiths sit in terror while Joe orchestrates the sharing of Kentucky Fried Chicken, mashed potatoes, and coleslaw. Together with the plastic cups and utensils, which reinforce the temporary, fleeting quality of food for this family, this dining scene is a far cry from the massive turkey, finery, and familial harmony of Rockwell's image. As the meal devolves into barbaric violence, Dottie is confronted with the reality of her broken family. She turns to murderous rage, and despite her repeated sexual exploitation by Killer Joe, she has him at gunpoint at the end of the play. She asserts the power of her body (to give birth) and her agency as the arbiter of who lives and who dies. In these ways, Letts upends any presumed connection between the disabled body and victimhood, challenging audiences to see beyond such stereotypes.

Disability and *Killer Joe* Twenty-Five Years Later

In the summer of 2018, Trafalgar Studios staged a revival of *Killer Joe* on the twenty-fifth anniversary of its premiere. Critical opinions ranged on this production from praising Orlando Bloom's performance as Killer Joe to finding fault with the cast's inconsistent Southern accents and the set's overwhelming sound effects. As one review noted, "None of the British cast seems particularly comfortable with the Texan milieu," and the critic for *The Guardian* concluded that "[Director] Simon Evans's production overplays the atmospheric thunder and lightning."[14] Several others lambasted the play's troubling gender politics.

For Paul Taylor, its sexual violence "shades queasily into the exploitative," making one "shudder at the play rather than with it." And Tom Bano found this revival particularly offensive in the context of the Me Too movement: "There is nothing remotely feminist, empowering or timely in watching a woman forced to simulate oral sex on a chicken leg in a production written and directed by men . . . Perhaps 20 years ago, Letts might have been able to argue that there was a point to watching a 22-year-old virgin with learning difficulties being ordered by a man to strip slowly before he has sex with her. In the current climate, though, it hardly needs restating that there are nasty men out there, and they will manipulate and beat and rape women."

Of course, this assessment raises a number of questions. Not even Bano would argue that the play endorses such violence, so what does Letts hope to achieve through such disturbing moments? Wasn't harassment center stage the year Letts wrote the play? In 1991, Anita Hill testified that Supreme Court nominee Clarence Thomas sexually harassed her when she worked for him at both the Department of Education and the Equal Employment Opportunity Commission. These televised hearings and the subsequent treatment of Hill suggested a need for social and political action. As such, can't we read *Killer Joe's* disturbing portrait of misogynistic violence as an indictment of a culture that refused to recognize the realities of patriarchal power structures and sexual abuse at the time?

It is striking that disability remains largely absent from these reviews—despite the extent to which the production foregrounds it. Trafalgar Studios is a relatively small venue in the West End of London. Three hundred people can barely squeeze into its cramped seats, yet this tight space replicated the quarters of the Smith trailer quite effectively. The stage itself spilled into the front few rows, requiring many ticket holders to walk across tufts of dead grass and dust to find their seats. From the second row, I could smell smoke from their cigarettes just as I caught the aroma of tuna casserole and Kentucky Fried Chicken. The intimacy of the space made you feel like one of the Smith's unseen neighbors peering through a window—uninvited but too riveted by the unfolding horrors to turn away.

About fifteen minutes before the performance, with the audience still looking for seats and deciding whether or not to buy a program, Dottie (Sophie Cookson) appears quietly on stage. She plays childlike games with herself such as kicking empty beer cans around the living room, talking to her doll, climbing over furniture, and ripping various items out of old newspapers. At one point, she discovers a dead mouse and studies it quizzically before placing the creature into the front pocket of her denim overalls. This moment, reminiscent of John Steinbeck's Lennie in *Of Mice and Men,* changes her demeanor. She walks with urgency toward the short hall leading to the bedrooms, lowers a rope ladder, and climbs onto the roof of the trailer. At this point, she begins a kind of ritual. She places the mouse in a cigar box, stands up, makes the sign of the cross, and looks toward the heavens. Lightening brightens the stage before everything goes dark. The play begins moments later with Chris (Adam Gillen) banging on the door.

This prelude reinforces some of the important themes of the play. Her games in the living room, for instance, take her from the television, into the kitchen, behind the couch, and back to the television again. This circular motion—like the setting itself—captures the way poverty and popular culture trap the Smith family. All of the characters move in circles, circumscribed by economic and moral impoverishment. Dottie's limited mobility also stems from disability. Her sleepwalking, abrupt perspicacity, and dreamy allusions to sexual abuse contribute to her depiction as developmentally disabled. Furthermore, her use of the rope ladder—a detail this production added to Letts's description of the setting—magnifies Dottie's presence. It gives her physical access to much of the action, and it puts the audience in the position of constantly surveilling her. When Chris and Ansel (Steffan Rhodri) discuss the murder and possible retainer with Joe, for example, she retreats to the roof to listen to music with headphones and to page through magazines. She returns to this place throughout the play, giving her disability a haunting presence and raising questions about what gets revealed to her and what remains obscured. The production, in other words, refuses to let the audience interpret any aspect of the drama apart from Dottie, her body, and the ongoing exploitation of her disability.

Finally, the rope ladder also functions as a metaphor for agency. No one throws Dottie a line (so to speak) or tries to rescue her in any way from the horrors of this trailer. She makes her own way to the roof, just as she chooses to end the lives of the Smith men and possibly Joe. Any surprise in the closing moments comes from the way audiences have underestimated her agency and capability. In these ways, the 2018 production emphasizes some of the disability politics that can be found in the play. It challenges viewers to understand Dottie's trajectory in terms of a culture that continues to marginalize, misunderstand, and even exploit disability.

If the critical response to this production is any indication, however, *Killer Joe* speaks to pressing concerns today. The play, written one year after the landmark Americans with Disabilities Act of 1990, certainly raised questions about the stigma associated with disability in America at the time. Letts was challenging audiences to rethink their assumptions about the labels that defined and limited difference. Likewise, the social realities of poverty and prejudice needed attention, and for Letts, art could play a crucial role in these efforts. It could snap the audience out of the kind of complacency encouraged by television and popular culture. Yet silence continues to surround so many instances of sexual abuse, and the poor and disabled still struggle for recognition and fairness. Perhaps the play's relevance at this contemporary moment—its power to disturb, provoke, and engage—stems from the recognition that the issues of disability bias and systemic poverty that haunted 1990s America continue to do so.

In these ways, Letts can be seen as participating in some of the goals of the disability theater movement. He is not disabled. His production notes do not insist on hiring a disabled actor to play Dottie, nor did he view himself as a disability activist while writing the play. Some critics can easily point to these facts as limitations, and they raise legitimate questions about the extent of Letts's investment in the sociopolitical dimensions of disability activism. By associating him with this movement ideologically, I do not mean to privilege a nondisabled playwright over the work celebrated in Lewis's *Beyond Victims and Villains*, for example. I suspect Letts would readily agree that disabled artists and playwrights need to be given a more prominent voice in American theater. Instead, I wish to position *Killer Joe* alongside works such as *The Glass Menagerie* and *As I Lay Dying* as having a valuable place in the discussion of disability and theater. Disability has been part of nondisabled fiction throughout American history—for better or worse—yet both the strengths and the limitations of these efforts can facilitate important discussions about bias among students, scholars, and theatergoers. It is my hope that the ongoing popularity of *Killer Joe* can contribute to these conversations, raising issues central to the disability theater movement and activism.

CHAPTER 3

Conspiracy Theories and Lost Children
in *Bug* and *The X-Files*

In the fifth season of *The X-Files,* federal agent Fox Mulder (David Duchovny) finds himself strapped to a hospital bed for psychiatric evaluation: "Five years together. You must have seen this coming," he quips to his partner Dana Scully (Gillian Anderson) ("Folie à Deux"). Mental illness looms large in the series, but it tends to function as misdirection. Whether through "spooky" Mulder's reputation for being "out there," the Lone Gunmen's conspiracy theories, or the general view of alien abductees as crackpots, *The X-Files* uses characters routinely dismissed as "crazy" to locate truth in the strange and the paranoid. The protagonist in "Duane Barry," for example, takes several people hostage after escaping from a mental hospital, yet his story of repeated abductions in-spires one hostage to tell him: "I just want to say that I believe you." The show's creator, Chris Carter, discusses the strategy behind these moments in the DVD commentary to "Fallen Angel": "It's a journey for Mulder and Scully to see— and for the audience to see—that these people who are crying wolf might be doing it for a reason . . . that they may be credible, seeing and knowing things that we don't." Just as the reasons for crying wolf often involve government conspiracies, Mulder and Scully's investigations also uncover profound social inequities at the heart of American culture. The oppressiveness and alienation of systemic poverty offer one example of this, and these economic narratives suggest that the real danger of conspiracy theories does not come from believ-ing in aliens per se but in allowing these theories to deflect from social problems that demand action.

While *The X-Files* emerged as one of the most popular and influential tele-vision series in the 1990s, Tracy Letts was writing and revising his second play,

Bug. The work premiered in London in 1996, and he spent the next decade revising it for various productions. One of the great innovations of *Bug* involves its preoccupation with the unseen. Specifically, its psychological exploration of paranoia continually navigates between the real and the imaginary, the factual and the fantastical. One never sees a bug onstage, and throughout most of the play, the sound of insects can be attributed to either the air conditioner, a distant helicopter, or the hum of traffic. Yet the actors playing Agnes White and Peter Evans respond visibly to the supposed infestation. They swat the air, squish bugs with their fingers, and scratch skin. As Uni Chaudhuri notes in her discussion of the play, "Watching other people scratching themselves can cause people to start feeling an itch themselves" (332), and this social contagion— much like one's response to a yawn—establishes a physiological connection to the drama. One's body becomes convinced of the protagonists' claims. These elements force viewers to share in Peter and Agnes's paranoid mindset, enabling Letts to capture both the appeal of and problem with conspiracy theories. Despite providing answers and comfort for the disenfranchised, conspiracy theories ultimately prove palliative. They provide no meaningful way to bring about social change.

Throughout *Bug* and *The X-Files,* conspiracy theories are also linked with grieving for abducted, abandoned, or dead children. Agnes's son, Lloyd, was kidnapped from a grocery store nearly ten years earlier, and she convinces herself that his disappearance is part of a government experiment to breed scientifically engineered bugs in her body. Fox Mulder constructs a similar narrative about loss. Once he learns about his sister's abduction through regression hypnosis, he links it with a government plot to hide the existence of extraterrestrial life from the public. For both Agnes and Mulder, conspiracy theories provide solace. They help make sense of profound loss. They offer answers for the inconceivable, such as the abduction or death of a child, and they provide an epic narrative for trauma. Personal tragedies can often feel inconsequential in the broader context of day-to-day life, yet conspiracy theories give a grandeur to individual loss. They enable these protagonists to craft intricate stories whose scope matches the depth of their suffering.

At the same time, *Bug* and *The X-Files* use the conspiracy genre—as opposed to conspiracy theories themselves—as a vehicle for cultural critique. Its narratives about lost children, either among the working poor or among middle-class families victimized by a working-class predator, draw attention to the socioeconomic conditions facilitating exploitation, and they challenge audiences to recognize the dangers of systemic poverty. Beginning with an overview of the conspiracy genre, this chapter examines the link between poverty and abduction in *Bug* and *The X-Files.* Ultimately, Letts's play and Carter's series use missing children to represent the forgotten poor and the risks of not seeing social inequality as a social crisis. Confronting the truth about these abductions, these works suggest, requires confronting uncomfortable truths about American society more broadly. It requires the individual to do something about injustice.

Conspiracy Narratives and Economic Hardship

Most scholars consider the 1960s a turning point in conspiracy culture as greater disillusionment with the U.S. government emerged after the assassinations of John and Robert Kennedy, Martin Luther King, Jr., and Malcom X. According to Peter Knight, the aftermath of these deaths made conspiracy theories "a regular feature of everyday political and cultural life, not so much an occasional outburst of countersubversive invective as part and parcel of many people's normal way of thinking about who they are and how the world works" (2). Indeed, a general distrust of the powers that be took hold by the end of the decade, and this mindset dovetailed with the disaffection of the countercultural movement. Whether through protests against the Vietnam War, the start of the environmental movement, the rallying cry against patriarchal oppression, or the beginning of the gay rights movement, these efforts forged an antiestablishment sensibility that resonated with millions. It considered white, heterosexist, male-dominated power structures to be the problem. It encouraged skepticism and distrust. And it radically shifted the way Americans perceived the government between the 1960s and 1990s. Prior to 1960, national polls revealed that 75 percent of Americans trusted the government, but that number would drop to 25 percent by 1994 (Knight 36). By the 1990s, in other words, conspiracy theory had moved from the fringes to the mainstream, characterizing the way most Americans viewed the government.

Theories about secret plots and cover-ups, as Theodore Zlolkowski notes, have found their artistic counterpart in the conspiracy genre (4). This genre typically features protagonists joined together by a sense of alienation,[1] placing them on a quest to uncover and destroy a mysterious agenda that threatens them and their society. According to Adrian Wisnicki, these narratives have six distinct characteristics: 1) a conspiracy theorist, 2) a paranoid subject, 3) the "hidden hand," 4) inaccessible authorities, 5) men plotting to defraud, and 6) a vanishing subject. The conspiracy theorist (a descendant of the literary detective) and paranoid subject offer a hypothesis that makes sense of and provides a means for resisting the threats posed by a conspiracy. This secret plot tends to be masterminded by inaccessible authorities or an oppressive group, such as the government or military, and oftentimes one character, or "hidden hand," "stands behind the scenes and guides events or the lives of other characters"

(Wisnicki 16). Although a plot to defraud in Victorian literature might involve, for example, two men planning to steal a widow's fortune, contemporary conspiracy narratives regularly feature governments and corporations obfuscating the truth for financial, social, or political gain. Finally, the vanishing subject refers to "a figure who somehow disappears in response to the oppression/surveillance of the authorities" (16). These vanishing figures remain relatively undefined, allowing other characters—as well as the audience—to interpret their significance.

The neatness of these characteristics, however, raises questions about the genre's effectiveness for political engagement. As many scholars have noted, the conspiracy genre is often a response to the lack of closure and unity in postmodernism, instead offering the assertion that everything is interconnected and explainable. According to Samuel Coale, "conspiracy as a fictional structure converts a cosmos of contingency and chance into a more rational realm of devious plot and secretive performance, thereby attempting to ground the mysteries and ambiguities of postmodernism in some kind of recognizable framework" (6). This contrast with postmodernism highlights the potential limitations of the genre. While conspiracy narratives often draw attention to social problems, suggesting the desire for a better world, they tend to revolve around "systemic investigation, exposure, and elimination." They fail, as Mark Fenster has argued, "to inform us how to move from the end of the uncovered plot to the beginning of a political movement" (289).[2] Postmodern fiction, by contrast, rejects the false comforts of conspiracy culture. It portrays this ideology as another form of entrapment by fostering a sense of alienation and invisibility that "make effective resistance (or separation) impossible" (McClure 258).

Despite this critique of conspiratorial connectivity, other scholars consider this genre an effective tool for addressing issues such as economic inequality.[3] According to David Kelman, conspiracy theories do not merely reflect contemporary crises; they provide "the essential narrative structure of any political articulation. In short, an attention to the narrative structure of conspiracy theories shows that every political narrative must tell the story of an illegitimate force that is undermining the legitimacy of an official or hegemonic discourse" (9). This tension between a rogue challenging force and dominant modes of power resonates with the conspiracy genre's investment in exposing economic exploitation. Many scholars have discussed the important link between financial instability and conspiracy ideology. Even though Richard Hofstadter's famous essay "The Paranoid Style in American Politics" primarily focuses on ethnic and religious conflict as the wellspring of paranoia, for example, he acknowledges class as a mobilizing force as well: "Feeling that they have no access to political bargaining or making of decisions, [the dispossessed] find their original conception of the world of power as omnipotent, sinister, and malicious fully confirmed" (39). Knight finds economic inequity particularly important for understanding the conspiracy mindset of the 1990s. The widening gap between the wealthy and poor coupled with declining wages in the middle class inspired many in the "formerly secure mainstream . . . [to turn] to the language and logic of extreme politics." As he explains, deregulation offered greater flexibility to corporate America, but "flexibility for corporations often means insecurity for workers" (40). Indeed, as Colin Harrison observes, "America may have been richer, but its citizens were more divided and more insecure" (7). By 1999, for example, "half of the nation's income was earned by the top fifth of the population while the bottom fifth took only 4.2 per cent" (Harrison 7). These conditions fostered feelings of disenfranchisement and powerlessness, enhancing the appeal of conspiracies to provide a scapegoat for socioeconomic hardships.

Bug and The X-Files tap into this intersection between conspiracy theory and oppressive class hierarchies through their depiction of working-poor life in 1990s America. Poverty circumscribes both Letts's characters and the destitute seeking Mulder and Scully's help. Conspiracy theories only fuel this oppression by tacitly condoning the status quo and by deflecting attention away from social problems. Although both Letts's play and Carter's series acknowledge the psychological appeal of such theories, they do so to highlight their failure to inspire political action. Bug and The X-Files thus use the conspiracy genre to critique the way this ideology perpetuates economic inequity, and the vanishing child, in particular, emerges as an image for the nation's failure to "see" the problems of poverty and ultimately to do something about it.

"Put it together. The pieces fit.": Conspiracy Culture, Loss, and Poverty in Bug

Letts's Bug focuses on the relationship between two characters who turn to conspiracy theories as a way of coping with loneliness, loss, and economic hardship. After the abduction of her six-year-old son and the incarceration of her abusive ex-husband, Agnes White withdraws from the world. She takes refuge in a motel room outside of Oklahoma City, works a dead-end job as a waitress, drinks in excess, freebases cocaine, and appears to have only one friend, a lesbian coworker named R.C. One night, Agnes begins a romance with Peter, a handsome stranger from the bar, and she soon learns that this Gulf War veteran has recently gone AWOL from a military hospital. Peter claims to be the victim of a secret government program to test various technologies, chemical weapons, diseases, and drugs on soldiers. He soon becomes convinced of an insect infestation in Agnes's room, which he attributes to egg sacs that have been implanted under his skin by the military. In many respects, Bug maps Agnes's descent into Peter's paranoid view of the world. Their shared delusions create a sense of belonging (to each other). They provide answers to the loss of her son and the loss of Peter's sanity. And they give Peter and Agnes a central role in a government plot to hatch experimental bugs that will infest the planet. This movement from victims to heroes, from marginalized poor to lynchpins in an international conspiracy, highlights the extent to which the working poor feel invisible in America. Peter and Agnes rely on conspiracy theories for some degree of recognition. Ultimately, Letts uses the conspiracy genre to expose the flaws of this ideology. Peter and Agnes lock themselves inside a motel room, shut off from the outside world, and this insularity reflects the failure of conspiracy theories to inspire social change. This presentation of paranoia also calls attention to the harmfulness of economic inequity, and the culminating violence of the play—with both characters immolating themselves to save the world—serves as a warning about the dangers of maintaining hierarchies that disenfranchise so many.

Although Peter's unwavering conviction in conspiracy theories might give even Fox Mulder pause, these extreme beliefs mirror the extent of Peter's alienation. He references the medical experiments of Edgewood and Tuskegee,[4] mind control, U.S. collaboration with Nazi scientists, surveillance, domestic terrorism, chemical poisoning, Gulf War syndrome, abductions, implants, aliens, and robots masquerading as humans. As Bigsby points out, there is an unnerving truth to many of Peter's claims, and the bizarreness of the play "is outdone by reality. Letts was in Oklahoma at the time of the bombing, which led him to become interested in people who had 'slipped out of the matrix' and desired to make sense of the event by locating it within a larger story" (*Twenty-First*, 104). The power of *Bug* does not come from the underlying truth in some of these assertions, however. It comes from the way conspiracies reflect a profound need among the dispossessed. They offer this group validation by acknowledging their struggles and by placing their lives, which mainstream society often ignores, at the center of contemporary society.

Peter, for example, relies on conspiracy theories to mitigate the depth of his social and familial isolation, but they serve only to marginalize him further. He admits that he has no place to go, and in asking for Agnes's friendship, he explains, "I'm just trying to make a connection" (Letts 13). This isolation stems from his recent break with the Army. After serving in the Gulf War and spending four years in a military psychiatric hospital, Peter decides to go AWOL. This decision leaves him rootless and penniless, for he viewed the Army both as his family and as a path to a lifelong career. Even though he believes himself to be a victim of medical and technological experiments by the military, the loss of this family removes him from the community he has relied on for self-definition. It also parallels the absence of his biological family. His mother died at a young age, and his father is a preacher without a congregation or church.

This career mirrors Peter's own status. He has lost his congregation in the military. He has neither a home (church) nor a source of income. And he preaches conspiracy ideology in the hopes of finding converts. At several points in the play, Agnes challenges his ideas, recognizing that this paranoid mindset may be an attempt to reestablish his identity as a soldier: "I'm just playin' devil's advocate here . . . Maybe you're just lookin' for a connection to the army" (42). For Letts, this moment underscores the palliative nature of conspiracy culture. It appears to connect Peter with others, such as veteran Timothy McVeigh, whom he says is the other recipient of a "subcutaneous . . . computer chip" (48), yet this "community" is artificial. Peter has never met McVeigh. In essence, Peter replaces real connections to family, fellow soldiers, and women with the extremist violence of the Oklahoma City bombing. The inexplicable horrors of that attack become a way for him to understand the horrific losses in his own life. They enable him to blame his own madness and feelings of violence on the government. Like the conviction that he is under constant surveillance, these beliefs offer him a narrative of self-importance that mitigates his loneliness.

Agnes's isolation stems from poverty and familial loss as well. As a waitress in a dive nightclub, she makes just enough money to pay for a motel room and a steady stream of drugs and alcohol. Agnes cannot afford many consumer goods, an apartment, or a ticket out of town—which makes her vulnerable to her ex-husband Goss's harassment. Her furnished room with its temperamental air conditioner captures the limitations of this working-poor life. She may take a certain satisfaction in the motel's "maid service," but she admits that she cannot pay all of her expenses. At one point, Goss even recalls their marriage in terms of economic hardship: "I drove [a sausage truck] twenty hours a day sometimes, so I could feed my wife and my kid" (Letts 31). Agnes's literal poverty also becomes a metaphor for her emotional losses. She hoped marriage and motherhood would give her a sense of belonging, but that proved not to be the case: "I just get sick of it, my lousy life, laundromats and grocery stores, dumb marriages and lost kids" (40). Economic hardship parallels the pain of broken families.

Just as marriage proved disappointing and dangerous—Goss nearly killed her once in a drunken rage (18)—the abduction of her son, Lloyd, remains an ongoing source of anguish. Nearly ten years ago, "he was with me, in the grocery store [. . .] in the cart . . . I forgot to get an onion . . . I went back for an onion, and left him in the cart . . . I came back to the cart, and he . . . he was just . . . he was gone" (50). Not surprisingly, when R.C. offers to protect her from Peter, Agnes protests: "You come in here and try to take away the only thing in the world I have, that's mine. Why can't I have one thing?" (28, 39). As her motel residence suggests, Agnes has nothing. She wants this relationship to compensate for the emotional, economic, and material deficits in her life. She hopes that having "one thing" will make the mundane routines of life, like doing laundry and shopping for groceries, bearable.

Amid the pain of lost children and poverty, conspiracy ideology emerges as both a coping mechanism and an ironic means for maintaining hierarchies that erase the poor. Through her gradual acceptance of Peter's mindset, Agnes begins to view her friendship with R.C. as part of a government plot. Specifically, R.C. and her partner, Lavoice, are fighting a seemingly hopeless custody battle for Lavoice's child: "I don't think the state's too hot on reuniting children with their beautiful lesbian mothers" (9). The surprise victory, however, heightens Agnes's sense of injustice. On one level, it represents her own fears of insignificance. The legal system grants R.C. and Lavoice the kind of family denied to Agnes. Despite their friendship, Agnes cannot understand how a homophobic state could help two lesbians and not her: "I just can't believe it, not in Oklahoma" (37). Unable to reconcile the disparity between her losses and R.C.'s gains, Agnes attributes it to a broader conspiracy: "The kid, Lavoice's boy, they gave her Lavoice's boy, they never woulda done that, but she brought the bugs to me in exchange for Lavoice's son" (51). Interestingly, this view of herself as host or queen bug lessens her guilt about Lloyd. It shifts the blame for the abduction from herself to governmental forces outside of her control. Her ability to be a mother again also hinges on this theory being true, for Agnes can now view herself as exceptional: "I'm the supermother. I'm the super-mother. I'm the supermother" (52). As the repetition and the hyphen suggest, conspiracy enables Agnes to reimagine herself as a good mother and to view her insect progeny as too attached to leave: "They wouldn't leave us, they'd never leave us . . . so they're coming in here, these people, to kill us, and send the bugs out, out into the world, the world" (52). Conspiracy theories thus mitigate this loss by restoring her maternal identity and providing her with children that will not disappear.

While the abduction of Agnes's son becomes a metaphor for the erasure of Americans trapped by poverty, Letts also uses it to expose conspiracy ideology as perpetuating harmful class hierarchies. Agnes recalls that the FBI and police "wouldn't help" find her son, and just as the legal system never protected her from Goss ("I'd get another court order if I thought it'd do any—"), both details capture her sense of insignificance within broader social institutions (50, 18). The decision to "hermitize" herself on the margins of Oklahoma City reflects this sense of erasure as well, for her isolation dovetails with the realization that society does not care (9). In the final moments of the play, she and Peter weave an intricate theory that magnifies their place in society. It provides a narrative for the inexplicable by removing the mystery surrounding some of the most difficult aspects of living—lost love, broken relationships, and missing children. It validates the depth of her loss. And it suggests that she and those in her socioeconomic circle matter. Though their narrative captures the fundamental appeal of conspiracy theories, it also highlights the tragedy of this ideology. Such a story offers Agnes no path for change or growth. Instead, she finds herself locked inside a motel room, walls covered in foil, contemplating suicide.

According to Peter, the driving force behind these secret experiments is maintaining the status quo, and Letts uses this theory to underscore his central message about economic inequity:

> PETER: a consortium of bankers, industrialists, corporate CEOs, and politicians [in the 1950s] . . . drew up a plan for maintaining the status quo . . . It's *the way things are*. It's the rich get richer, and the poor poorer. It's a piece of shit, but you got to where you kind of liked it . . . They devised a plan to manipulate technology, economics, the media, population control, world religion, to keep things *the way they are*. (48)

Peter's narrative gets increasingly convoluted as he tries to explain the origins of brainwashing bugs, but his commentary about a class system that thrives on inequality resonates. It is a moment of moral and social clarity in the play. As the audience has been watching this relationship unfold in a grimy motel room, poverty emerges as one of the primary causes of their entrapment. Their use of drugs and alcohol for escapist pleasure—like Goss's desire to watch TV— fits Peter's assessment that "you got to where you kind of liked it." Poverty is rooted in limited resources as well as a tacit acceptance of hierarches that disenfranchise one group for the benefit of another. For Letts, the conspiracy genre becomes an ideal vehicle for exposing the palliative nature of conspiracy theories. They reduce everyone to victims of outside forces, and as such, they perpetuate the status quo by discouraging social action. Peter and Agnes turn inward, and their gestures at resistance remain largely private. Ultimately, Letts uses their immolation to suggest that such socioeconomic inequities have explosive consequences for the nation.

Lost Children and the Forgotten Poor in *The X-Files*

From 1992 to 2002 (as well as the current revivals in 2016 and 2018), *The X-Files* placed its protagonists, FBI agents Fox Mulder and Dana Scully, at the center of a government conspiracy to hide the truth about extraterrestrial life, alien abductions, the engineering of alien–human hybrids, and a host of other horrors. However, not every installment focused on this mythology. In the tradition of *The Twilight Zone* and *Kolchak: The Night Stalker*, *The X-Files* offered monster-of-the-week episodes, which featured various creatures such as ancient insects, cockroaches, werewolves, vampires, golems, zombies, and other mutants. Even these standalone episodes often revealed government agents and the military to be responsible for varying degrees of mayhem and deception. The fundamental tension in *The X-Files* involves the juxtaposition of Mulder's unquestioning belief in conspiracy ideology and supernatural phenomena with Scully's rational, scientific sensibility as a medical doctor. This dichotomy functions largely as sleight of hand, for science rarely triumphs in the show. It ends up supporting Mulder's paranoia by inviting audiences to find answers in conspiracy theories as well, much the way Agnes does with Peter's ideas in *Bug*. In the world of *The X-Files,* the government is the problem. It tests biological weapons on the public, works closely with former Nazi scientists, stages alien abductions, assassinates people with impunity, impregnates women through rape to breed alien–human hybrids, and colludes with alien forces intent on colonizing the planet. As Douglas Kellner notes, the series depicts government agencies and the military as "filled with individuals who carry out villainous actions and constitute a threat to traditional humanistic moral values and human life itself" (218). In this context, conspiracy ideology becomes the only reasonable lens for viewing modern American life.

The X-Files is also preoccupied with missing children. Mulder's driving motivation is the loss of his sister. As he explains in the pilot episode, nothing matters more than finding out the truth about Samantha's abduction. Yet Mulder has only the vaguest recollection of what happened. With the Watergate hearings on television, his parents at a party next door, and the board game Stratego on the living room floor, he recalls a bright light carrying her away. It is a moment of utter paralysis that foreshadows the way this loss will freeze him in time. Neither eyewitness accounts nor forensic evidence can confirm his story. In fact, from the beginning of the series, *The X-Files* raises doubts about Mulder's account through both Scully's scientific skepticism ("What I find fantastic is any notion that there are answers beyond the realm of science") and the fact that this memory can only be recalled through "deep regression hypnosis" ("Pilot"). Such uncertainty pushes Mulder into an obscure branch of the FBI called the X-Files—a potpourri of forgotten, unsolved cases involving paranormal phenomena and alien abductions. These strange cases, like the ambiguity surrounding Samantha's abduction, become vehicles for the series to use lost children as metaphors for uncomfortable truths about American culture that people see but do not want to believe.

Many scholars have noted the way extraterrestrials or aliens represent the theme of alienation in *The X-Files*. Kellner, for example, views the alien "as a figure for what humans have become in an era in which individuals no longer feel that they control their own destiny, in which their own bodies mutate out of control, and their minds and bodies are invaded with new societal, techno-logical, and political forces" (228). Such feelings of vulnerability inspire many characters in *The X-Files* to turn to conspiracy theories for answers, and this shared ideology often forges connections among people of different socioeco-nomic and ethnic backgrounds. As Teresa Gellar has observed, the show's ex-ploration of social alienation includes "disenfranchised groups such as POWs from the Vietnam War and undocumented immigrants" (24), and Mulder and Scully's efforts on their behalf demonstrate an earnest investment in justice. These investigations also challenge the kind of binaries that often justify the marginalization of certain groups. For Paul Cantor, such divisions are critical for the nation-state, which needs to create "aliens" to maintain power: "Na-tionalism rests on simplistic polarizations between *us* and *them* and above all develops a notion of distinct national identity, often based on ideas of cultural homogeneity, monolingualism, and even racial purity" (123). The alienating impact of the nation-state stems largely from "its attempt to impose economic and bureaucratic rationality on its citizens; it alienates them from their ethnic heritage, their regional ties, their communal traditions, and above all their myths—which the nation-state views as archaic sources of irrationality that must be eliminated for the sake of progress" (Cantor 190). This pressure for cultural uniformity, in other words, exacerbates the isolation and vulnerability of the immigrant, the outsider, and the alien.

Certainly, *The X-Files* includes ethnic identity in its portrait of alienation in the modern world,[5] but far less attention has been paid to the show's explo-ration of class. While immigrant groups ("aliens") from Mexico, Haiti, Africa, China, and the like experience mistreatment because of their ethnicity, they also suffer from poverty. In "Hell Money," for example, Hsin (Michael Yama) begins gambling with his organs because he cannot afford medical treatment for his daughter's leukemia. Samuel Aboah (Willie Amakye) in "Teliko" can prey on poor black men because their deaths go largely unremarked outside of the black community: "young black men are dying and . . . nobody cares." And poverty utterly shapes the lives of the Native Americans living on the Trego Indian Reservation in "Shapes." Other episodes use class resentment as a back-drop. In "Drive" (6.2), for example, Patrick Crump (Bryan Cranston) believes that the "Jew FBI" has been secretly experimenting on him and his wife, in part because the government views poor people as expendable. Jenny Uphouse (Gina Mastrogiacomo) in "Chimera" views her affair with the sheriff as a kind of revenge against the snobbery of middle-class suburban wives. She might not get access to their nice homes, but sex at least provides a temporary opportunity to feel superior. "Pusher" features a killer, Robert Modell (Robert Wisden), who can impose his will on others. As an unremarkable student with a community college education, Modell seems capable only of getting a job as a convenience store clerk, and this mundane, working-class life makes him desperate for recognition. Pushing his will onto others becomes an inversion of the way external forces, such as limited opportunities, have determined the course of his life. And "Theef" involves a poor Southern man who uses voodoo to enact revenge on a wealthy doctor for euthanizing his daughter. Hexes and curses are the only weapons he has against the privilege and status of people like Dr. Wieder (James Morrison).

As with Tracy Letts's *Bug*, some of the most provocative uses of poverty in *The X-Files* come from its juxtaposition of the lost child motif with its ability to expose conspiracy ideology as an obstacle to social change. A number of episodes such as "Oubliette," "Paper Hearts," "Sein und Zeit," and "Closure" establish a connection between lost children and economic hardship, making abduction a metaphor for the invisible poor and conspiracy theory an escape from the real impact of economic injustice in America. These episodes tend to place missing children at the center of broader narratives about poverty, forcing Mulder and Scully to confront their own privilege as they encounter the poor and destitute. Even when the abducted child is middle-class, as with Samantha Mulder in "Paper Hearts" and "Closure" or Amy Jacobs in "Oubliette," the threat tends to come from working-class predators, suggesting a need to address some of the profound social problems and class resentments at the heart of American society. Ultimately, through missing children, Mulder and Scully must engage with people of different socioeconomic backgrounds to solve a case, and in some instances they must act on their behalf. In doing so, they demonstrate the need to recognize the forces that marginalize people— particularly poverty—and invite audiences to assume a shared responsibility for these groups as well.

Written by Charles Grant Craig, "Oubliette" juxtaposes two child abduction stories in its examination of class tensions in the United States. At the exact moment of Amy Jacobs's (Jewel Staite's) kidnapping in suburban Seattle, a fast food waitress named Lucy Householder (Tracey Ellis) collapses across town with a severe nose bleed, muttering the words of the kidnapper and bleeding Amy's blood. Mulder, intrigued by this strange connection, seeks out Lucy's help in finding the missing girl. He soon discovers that Lucy had been kidnapped as a child, held captive in a basement, and sexually abused for years. Now, she seems to be reliving this abduction vicariously through Amy. The contrast between these young women establishes the different values associated with middle-class and working-class life. Amy is an attractive, articulate fifteen-year-old girl who appears to be a good student (as suggested by the books on her nightstand) and a model teenager, sharing a room with her baby sister and going to bed by ten o'clock. She lives in a suburban home with a spacious front yard and tastefully decorated rooms. Her bedroom contains countless stuffed animals, books, toys, and a stereo. In the opening sequence, both she and her sister sleep snugly under thick comforters, and the open window suggests the family's confidence in the security promised by suburbia. They do not expect a working-class photographer's assistant to climb through the window and take their daughter. As Mrs. Jacobs (Sidonie Boll) explains in a daze, "Who could take somebody who wasn't theirs?" In many ways, however, the episode is about who takes things in America, and at whose expense. Amy's abduction garners the full resources of local police and the FBI. No expense is spared to find her, for Amy represents the values of white suburbia—values that must be protected from the likes of working-class predators.

By contrast, Lucy's abduction experience has driven her to illegal, self-destructive behaviors, making her representative of an underclass that mainstream America would like to forget. The title, "Oubliette," refers to the dark cellar where sexual predator Carl Wade (Michael Chieffo) holds young girls captive, and this space becomes a haunting image for Lucy's experiences both as a victim of prolonged abuse and as a member of the working poor. With hunched shoulders and darting eyes, Lucy's body language communicates her sense of ongoing entrapment by past and present traumas. As Mulder notes, "She'd been held in the dark so long her eyes were hypersensitive to the light . . . She's thirteen years old here [in a video made shortly after her escape] and can barely string two words together." She subsequently turns to drugs and prostitution to cope. Like her status as a trainee at a fast food restaurant, Lucy's life in the Bright Angel Halfway House captures her financial and social instability. She is stuck between imprisonment and freedom, between a presumed middle-class childhood and a working-poor present, and between transitional housing and owning ("holding") a home as her last name suggests. At one point, Mulder comments that "it's amazing she's gotten anywhere in life," to which Scully replies: "Well, by most yardsticks, she hasn't." The yardstick here is a middle-class value system, and the episode suggests that those whose lives unfold outside of such standards tend not to be measured at all.

This contrast between Amy and Lucy also crafts the oubliette into an image for the hidden poor and for economic exploitation more broadly. Lucy's prominent role in this case draws attention to her life on the social margins. Local cops grumble about her "kind," convinced that poverty and a criminal past define her, and they have no interest in the forces that have produced and continue to limit Lucy. In this way, the quest to save Amy becomes a way of preserving middle-class values at the expense of the poor. Lucy's vicarious experiences make her a victim of this crime without any official support (apart from Mulder). Lucy's body bears Amy's scratches and bruises. She feels the same bone-chilling cold, desperate thirst, and blindness from being locked in the dark. This shared pain culminates in Wade's attempt to drown Amy. During this sequence, the camera cuts repeatedly to Lucy's face as she coughs up water, turns blue, and draws her final breath. Not only does the coroner find five liters of water in Lucy's lungs, but Amy walks away unscathed. As Scully summarizes: "There were no injuries . . . She didn't have a cut on her, and nobody wants to talk about that right now. Everyone is just relieved to have her back again, to have her safe." This moment underscores the class implications of the episode. A certain silence surrounds Lucy's death and the lives of the working poor more broadly. As her damaged body suggests, Lucy becomes an expendable resource for the middle-class suburban culture that Amy represents. Lucy is used to find, rescue, and spare Amy from the horrors of molestation and murder. Mulder may optimistically conclude that this sacrifice was "the only way she could escape, the only way she could forget what happened seventeen years ago. Finally the only way she could outrun Carl Wade." But she cannot outrun the limitations of her class. Clearly, the police and community are much happier substituting Amy for Lucy, and Lucy's erasure in death mirrors her social insignificance in life.

Finally, the connection between this case and Samantha Mulder's abduction reinforces the episode's message about economic inequity. Throughout the investigation, Mulder encourages Lucy to fight on Amy's behalf: "You're sharing her pain . . . Now [she] needs some of your strength . . . and you have to help her." This call to take a shared responsibility for others aligns with Mulder's theory about the case: "Wade's abduction of Amy triggered some kind of physical response in Lucy, some kind of empathic transference." This notion extends to the audience as well, for the episode challenges viewers to empathize with both Amy and Lucy. In fact, Mulder's empathy for Lucy focuses the audience's attention on the various hegemonic forces that have victimized her, most notably poverty and trauma. Even Scully's questions about Mulder's motives end up supporting his perspective: "You're becoming some kind of an empath yourself, Mulder." For Scully, this is a case of misplaced loyalties: "You are so sympathetic to Lucy, as a victim, like your sister, that you can't see her as a person who is capable of committing this crime." Mulder, however, proves to be right about this transference, and Scully's errors in judgement—from Lucy's innocence to the possibility of resuscitating Amy—include the importance of self-sacrifice as well. Lucy's extreme empathy saves Amy's life after all, and in this way, the show makes empathy a heroic act. Mulder models such behavior, demonstrating an indefatigable willingness to sacrifice himself for both Lucy and Amy. In rejecting Scully's reductionist view of his relationship with Lucy, Mulder argues that "motivations for behavior can be more complex and mysterious than tracing them back to one single childhood experience." His interest in the circumstances of her life transcends the personal. He recognizes the social factors that continue to trap Lucy, and his actions become an attempt to rectify some of this injustice.

The closing scene invites audiences to share in Mulder's and arguably Lucy's commitment to individual sacrifice. After looking through her childhood pictures, which capture moments of carefree innocence and happiness, Mulder moves from Lucy's bed to the window. The acts of sitting on her bed and looking out her window reflect the depth of his empathy. Like his decision to protect her from law enforcement, Mulder tries to occupy her spaces and to assume her perspective on the world. He might not have any experience with poverty, but he has done what no one else was willing to do—to understand and care for Lucy. In the final shot, with Scully now on the bed and Mulder at the window, the viewer's vantage point from the doorway does not reveal what Mulder sees, and this distance suggests that we have to earn that place at the window. We—the show's predominantly white, upper-middle-class viewership[6]—have to make efforts to see the struggles of people like Lucy. It is not enough to watch from a distance as one does with television. We have to enter the room and take the steps that lead to social change.

As with *Bug*, Vince Gilligan's "Paper Hearts" presents child abduction, in part, as an image for the dangers both of marginalizing the poor and of conspiracy ideology. The episode confronts Mulder with the possibility that a serial killer, not aliens, abducted his sister. The killer, John Lee Roche (Tom Noonan), is already serving a life sentence for his crimes, but when Mulder finds proof of three additional victims, he reopens the case. Roche, a door-to-door vacuum salesman in the 1970s and 1980s, used this job as an opportunity to kidnap, molest, and murder young girls. He preyed on middle-class suburban families in particular, and various details in the episode suggest an underlying class resentment on his part. When identifying one of the recently discovered victims, for example, he recalls that "I had her mother on the hook for an Electrovac Argosy, but at the last minute, she said 'thanks but no thanks.'" The brief acrimony in his tone offers a subtle reminder about the economic constraints of his working-class life. He relied on these sales for financial security, and to some extent, this anecdote suggests that he took this girl as a perverse compensation for the indignities of being a salesman.

Roche's access to these homes also offered vivid reminders of the contrast between his working-class life and that of the suburban middle class. Like Mulder's father, who bought a vacuum from Roche as a gift for his wife, these families could afford to buy appliances and spacious homes in affluent places such as Martha's Vineyard. By contrast, Roche's small, dingy apartment in Boston looked out onto an empty field and a bus graveyard. The rundown apartment building and the fact that a squatter appears to have taken residence in Roche's place imply the ongoing poverty of the surrounding neighborhood. Roche responded to this contrast by taking what was most valuable to these families: children. Abducting them not only shattered the presumed safety of such middle-class havens ("I was ready to kick the door in . . . It was unlocked. It was 1973. It was a different world back then."), but it also served as an ironic inversion of suburban migration. Middle-class or aspiring middle-class whites traditionally flocked to the suburbs to leave behind the presumed dangers of the city, such as poverty, crime, and ethnic diversity. Roche, however, brings some of these dangers to the suburbs, polluting the natural beauties of Martha's Vineyard with urban decay and violence.

Through its allusions to Lewis Carroll's (Charles Dodgson's) novel *Alice in Wonderland* (1865), "Paper Hearts" also captures the dangers of relying on master narratives, such as alien abductions and serial killers, that deflect attention from socioeconomic problems. The madness of Carroll's Hatter comes, in part, from the way he challenges both linguistic and social conventions. He poses a riddle without an answer. He offers wine when there is none. And he claims that a quarrel with Time has forced him to live perpetually at six o'clock—dooming him to host a tea party that will never end. In some ways, Roche embodies these behaviors, and the episode uses his madness to highlight middle-class America's unwillingness to confront the potential dangers of class hierarchies. Roche views himself as a kind of "Mad Hatter." He cuts heart shapes from the pajamas of his victims and keeps them in his copy of the novel. He too manipulates language, posing riddles to Mulder about the death of his sister and promising the truth about her abduction with no intention of revealing it. And he appears trapped in time, longing to relive his murderous impulses with one final victim. Though his actions are attributed to a mad perversity, his choice of victims—middle-class white girls—points to the economic subtext of the episode. The first body discovered in the episode has pajamas with a dollar sign woven into the shirt pocket, and though her father later explains its connection to the Tooth Fairy, the image implies a class dimension to these crimes. Even Roche's suit makes him appear nonthreatening both to the mother and daughter on the plane and, in footage edited from the final version, to the daycare provider whom he approaches in the guise of Fox Mulder. Roche, with his calm demeanor and soft-spoken eloquence, can pass as white-collar, and this sleight of hand prevents Mulder—as well as the audience—from considering the way class resentment fuels his pathology.

Ultimately, it is Mulder's desperate need for a master narrative that reveals belief in conspiracy theories as a kind of dangerous madness. This mindset makes him particularly vulnerable to Roche's story, for Mulder's instinct is to replace one extreme theory (alien abduction) with another (molestation and murder). When Scully questions Mulder's susceptibility to Roche's claims, he asks: "Do you believe that my sister was abducted by aliens? . . . Have you ever believed that? No. So what do you think happened to her?" This need for a concrete explanation not only isolates Mulder from Scully, but it also inspires professional and personal recklessness. Mulder removes Roche from jail, endangering his own life and giving him the opportunity to abduct another girl. As the episode suggests, a certain madness comes from both ignorance and knowledge. As one grieving father tells Mulder, "I used to think that missing was worse than dead because you never knew what happened. Now that I know, I'm glad my wife's not here. She got luckier." At the same time, there is also a madness in pursuing one theory after another for answers. Mulder abandons extraterrestrial terrors for the terrestrial here, but neither prove satisfying. Roche never reveals the truth about his final victim, and Mulder must live with this uncertainty. His flaw, much like Alice's—and thus the flaw of conspiracy culture more broadly—is the need to impose artificial order on chaos. In the closing scene, Mulder stares at the final heart in Roche's collection, and the unanswered questions (Who was the victim? Was it Samantha? Where is her body?) encapsulate the episode's message about such loss. Coping with the inexplicable can be one of the most trying, painful aspects of human existence, and it takes tremendous fortitude to do so.

In the seventh season of *The X-Files*, Chris Carter and Frank Spotnitz penned two episodes to resolve the Samantha storyline, and both "Sein und Zeit" and "Closure" link child abduction with the dangers of socioeconomic inequity and conspiracy theories. Once again, a serial killer emerges as a possible culprit for Samantha's abduction. The killer, a man who plays Santa Claus at Santa's Village in northern California, targets children that visit the park, later abducting them from their suburban homes and burying their bodies in a field. The suburban home of the most recent victim, Amber Lynn LaPierre, has the trappings of the middle class, with spacious rooms and matching furniture. By contrast, Santa is characterized as a working-poor man who preys on middle-class children. His cheap clothing (T-shirts and baggy pants), the retractable keychain on his belt that makes him resemble a janitor, and slovenly office, which contains video tapes of his victims, signal a meager existence. One encounter with an impatient parent implies some of this class tension as well. "Hey, buddy," the father snaps in exasperation, "The kids want to see Santa. What about it?" Santa's status as an employee exposes him to these types of indignities, and as with Roche, he exacts a steep price from these families.

These episodes also offer a microcosm of Mulder's problematic use of conspiracy theory through his mother's suicide. Like Peter from *Bug*, Mulder tries to explain her death through a string of conspiracy theories. As Mulder tells Scully, "She was afraid that they would do something like this to her [. . .] whoever took my sister. Look at this place. I mean it's like . . . It's all staged, the pills, the oven, the tape. It's like a bad movie script. They would . . . they would have come here, and they would have threatened her." None of this proves true, but after seven years of watching Mulder pursue his sister, the audience is willing to entertain such a possibility. We have been coaxed into a paranoid mindset through Mulder's journey. In this way, these episodes remind viewers of the psychological and emotional appeal of conspiracy culture. They replace the inexplicable and abstract with something tangible. Even Mulder concludes that he has relied on Samantha's abduction narrative to cope with loss: "All these visions that I've had have just been . . . they've been to help me cope, to help me deal with the loss." Not surprisingly, his instinct is to replace a conspiracy theory about alien abduction with a supernatural theory, and he claims that his sister was taken by Walk Ins—old spirits that protect children from pain by taking their souls into the starlight. As he did in "Paper Hearts," he substitutes one coping mechanism for another, but when Scully argues that Mrs. Mulder "was trying to tell you . . . to stop looking for your sister. She was just trying to take away your pain," he must confront this loss. It is a moment that allows him to fully experience and express grief. As such, these episodes point to the limits of the conspiracy theory. It holds pain at bay by redirecting one's focus onto intricate plots and deceptions. It doesn't allow for healing.

These episodes stop short of presenting Mulder as delusional, however, and in keeping with the broader mythology of the series, he finds evidence of the government's complicity in Samantha's abduction. He comes to believe that these Walk Ins spared her from torturous government experiments. He even gets to embrace her childlike spirit in the closing moments. Although this moment enables Mulder to maintain both his beliefs about the government and his faith in supernatural phenomena, the message about conspiracy ideology and catharsis remain the same. Conspiracy theories do not offer the kind of resolutions that enable healing. They prevent one from focusing on truths "in the real world," as Skinner notes, and some of these truths involve class hierarchies that perpetuate resentment and violence. Just as *The X-Files* gradually deconstructs some of the conspiracy theories surrounding Samantha's abduction, it uses the missing child motif in several episodes as a metaphor for the forgotten poor and for the dangers of not seeing the social problems that cause economic inequity. Confronting the truth about Samantha's and Amber's abductions requires, in part, understanding the forces that shaped this serial-killing Santa. As such, it also requires confronting uncomfortable truths about American culture more broadly.

Lost and Found in the Age of Conspiracy Culture

Just as Peter, Agnes, and Scully use microscopes to examine evidence, their desire to see the unseen invites questions about what and who gets overlooked in America. In a sense, *Bug* and several episodes of *The X-Files* give the audience a microscopic view into the lives of the working poor and their feelings of alienation and desperation. This kind of poverty proves to be fertile ground for conspiracy theories. Such theories provide solace, moving one from the margin to the center. They offer an escapist outlet for the hardships of daily life and explain the inexplicable—whether the loss of one's child or a lost sense of self. They do so, however, at the price of maintaining the status quo. By providing no meaningful solutions for social problems, conspiracy ideology reduces Agnes and Peter, for example, to victims of larger forces. It may function as a microscope for seeing previously hidden government plots and military secrets, but in truth, it is like the bug infestation that they fret over. Conspiracy ideology spreads and spreads, continually replacing one plot with another to avoid uncomfortable truths about modern life.

The infectious nature of conspiracy culture has only intensified in the twenty-first century, giving *Bug* and *The X-Files* a compelling resonance today. The Internet Age has made it easier than at any other point in history to embrace paranoia, to shut out dissenting voices and challenging viewpoints, and to find like-minded support for the most cynical and callous beliefs. This myopic insularity makes conspiracy theory believers particularly vulnerable to manipulation. Hackers can influence elections by spreading untruths. President Donald Trump can lie with impunity on a daily basis, dismissing facts as "fake news," and his administration can use conspiracy theories to justify draconian policies. In this climate, the conspiracy theory has made paranoia and intolerance the touchstone of American politics. And it has been weaponized to hurt the most vulnerable among us, whether by putting migrant children in cages at the Southern border or by attempting to roll back food stamps and other social services.

The conspiracy genre, by contrast, proves to be a particularly effective tool for exposing this ideology as part of the problem. It taps into the popularity of this thinking—with its simplistic view of the world (good/evil, us/them) and self-aggrandizing impulse—in order to comment on the need for social and political transformation. By using the vulnerability of missing children as an image for the working poor, the conspiracy genre in *Bug* and *The X-Files* challenges audiences to "see" those who have been alienated and to act on their behalf. The painful losses that afflict Agnes and Mulder require them to retread familiar ground to seek answers. As Agnes descends further into paranoid madness, her motel room becomes a relentless image for her social and psychological entrapment. Likewise, Mulder's encounters with abducted children—like the ongoing mythology of the series—expose him repeatedly to class inequities and tensions. In both cases, audiences are challenged to look more closely at these problems. They are asked to abandon the false comforts of conspiracy theories and to consider what responsibility they have for protecting the most vulnerable among us.

CHAPTER 4

Food, Culinary Justice, and Native American Identity in *August: Osage County*

When Tracy Letts was ten years old, his grandfather drowned himself, and his grandmother began a precipitous descent into drug addiction. More than thirty years later, these devastating events would become the inspiration for *August: Osage County*. In the play, family bonds foster a sense of belonging accompanied by deep-seated resentment. They embrace and suffocate, nurture and neglect. As suggested by the Weston family's inability or unwillingness to cook, the characters hunger for deeper connections with each other. Yet their failure to achieve intimacy, according to Letts, comments on the "very imperfect unit by which we govern and raise our species."[1] This subject matter situates *August: Osage County* in the tradition of great American family dramas, including Arthur Miller's *Death of a Salesman*, Lillian Hellman's *Little Foxes*, Edward Albee's *Who's Afraid of Virginia Woolf?*, and Beth Henley's *Crimes of the Heart*.[2] Mobilizing "the leitmotif of American theater"—family—allows Letts to craft a work about "everyone's home—a harrowing and hilarious portrait of the American family as our greatest blessing and our greatest curse" (Choate 105, 106).

This universality has social implications as well, and according to Bigsby, it enables the play to "[dissect] not just a family but a country . . . Letts himself has said, that his characters 'were representative of the country on some level,' the very name of the Westons echoing the promise once offered in the move west" (*Twenty-First,* 110–11). The West of the twenty-first century, however, provides nothing but stagnation, unfulfilled appetites, and exploitation. It is no accident that the Weston house has not been renovated since 1972. Taped window shades obscure "night or day" (19), and no one has used the stove in years. This stasis implies a broader social and moral decline, and Letts uses the family's relationship with Native American culture to examine ugly truths about colonialism and food production in America. Specifically, food highlights issues of injustice rooted in the colonial oppression of Indigenous people in the United States since the eighteenth century. Whether through the erasure of Cheyenne cuisine or reliance on environmentally harmful food practices, cooking and eating in the play point to the need for culinary justice rooted in indigeneity.

August: Osage County—which premiered at the Steppenwolf Theater Company in Chicago in 2007, transferred to Broadway, and earned the Pulitzer, Tony, and New York Drama Critics' Circle Awards in 2008—opens with Beverly Weston interviewing a Cheyenne woman, Johnna, for a housekeeping job. A disillusioned academic who published one notable book of poetry forty years earlier, Beverly has drowned his artistic and professional failings in alcohol. His alcoholism, together with his wife Violet's addiction to pills, have "made burdensome the maintenance of traditional American routine: paying of bills, purchase of goods, cleaning of clothes or carpets or crappers" (11). Their addictions have also kept them both from eating, so one of Johnna's primary duties is cooking. As Johnna quietly prepares meals and cleans, Violet's tongue gets sharper and meaner with each pill. Her racism becomes a tool to diminish the significance of Johnna's role in the house and of indigeneity more broadly ("What's wrong with 'Indian'? . . . Let's just call the dinosaurs 'Native Americans' while we're at it" [31].) Violet's cruelty also explains the distance between her and her three daughters. Only one, Ivy, has remained in Oklahoma, but her life as a single librarian who refuses to dress provocatively or wear makeup remains a source of consternation for Violet. Ivy's secret romance with Little Charles, her cousin, proves devastating when she discovers that they are actually siblings from her father's affair with Mattie Fae. Barbara, the eldest, lives in Colorado with her husband and fourteen-year-old daughter, Jean. Her husband's sexual affair with a student has effectively ended their marriage, and Jean, following in the addictive footsteps of her family, loses herself in marijuana and old movies. Finally, Karen, the youngest daughter at forty, has recently gotten engaged to Steve. She hopes to build a life with him in Florida, but his attempt to molest Jean casts doubt on their future.

The climax of the play occurs at a formal dinner (prepared by Johnna) after Beverly's funeral in which Violet uses "truth-telling" to demean her children (70). This truth-telling forces the sisters to confront the extent of their disconnection from one another. Neither Barbara nor Karen knows of Ivy's cervical cancer, for example, and Barbara has kept her marital troubles secret. In the end, the complete dissolution of the family occurs when Violet reveals that she knew about Beverly's plan to kill himself. He left a note with an invitation to call him at a local motel, but Violet—in order to prove her strength ("Who's stronger now, you son-of-a-bitch?!" [101])—waited so she could seize the contents of their safety deposit box. Disgusted by this callousness, Barbara abandons her mother, reducing Violet to a childlike state, and the play ends with her climbing to the attic on all fours to be comforted by Johnna.

The Westons tell the story of American decline in the twenty-first century. Just as Beverly recognized that something "was disappearing, had disappeared" in the United States, Barbara concludes, "This country, this experiment, America, this hubris: what a lament, if no one saw it go. Here today, gone tomorrow. Dissipation is actually much worse than cataclysm" (91). In many respects, *August: Osage County* examines the causes and symptoms of this dissipation through Johnna. Her working-poor status, cooking skills, and relationship with farming become emblematic of the exploitation of Native Americans. Meanwhile, the Westons' unwillingness to cook (or inability to cook well, in the case of Mattie Fae's notorious casserole) links their familial dissipation with a national one. They are rapturous over Johnna's traditional "American" meals—from Southern specialties such as biscuits and gravy to apple pie—yet these foods capture a nostalgic impulse to see the country in clichéd terms of bounty, progress, and community. Letts's portrait of the Westons suggests the opposite. Like this broken family, America is buckling under generations of economic inequity, racism, and the environmental harm caused by modern food production. This history also exposes the country's profound moral failing in our refusal to care for one another and the planet. Beginning with a discussion of the decolonial food movement, this chapter examines Letts's use of food—particularly the tension between home cooking and processed foods, vegetarianism and meat eating—to explore the legacy of Native American genocide and to critique culinary injustice as emblematic of the forces that continue to exploit people of color and the environment.

Food Studies, Decolonial Food Activism, and Contemporary Theatre

The interdisciplinary field of food studies, with roots in anthropology, history, and sociology, explores how eating choices communicate individual and cultural preferences. It interrogates the forces that shape food production, distribution, and disposal. And as Carole Counihan and Penny Van Esterik note, it supports the efforts of food activists "to end world hunger and to bring about universal access to nutritious and adequate food" (10). This perspective is echoed by Mustafa Koç, Jennifer Sumner, and Tony Winson in *Critical Perspectives in Food Studies,* which considers the field both an academic discipline and "a means to change society" (xii). Such activism also plays a central role in the decolonial food movement through its efforts to protect farmers and food-supply workers, to resist practices that harm the ecosystem, and to draw attention to culinary injustice. As Devon G. Peña, Luz Calvo, Pancho McFarland, and Gabriel R. Valle have noted, "many Indigenous peoples are said to have lost their food, foodways, and cuisines—heritage erased through veritable population extinctions or forgotten in the aftermath of the collapse and expulsion of entire regional Indigenous communities by the violent forces of settler colonial empires" (xvi–xvii). In other words, colonialism denied displaced populations access to their traditional modes of cooking and eating. The result was starvation, disease, and the replacement of healthy foods with harmful alternatives. According to Winona LaDuke, "the forced reliance on inadequate government rations, often called 'commodity foods,' only changed the starvation from quick and obvious to hidden and slow" (191).[3] This relationship between food and colonial history has inspired contemporary efforts to reclaim "lost" foodways. Indigenous communities in the twenty-first century "are recovering agricultural traditions linking past to present and future—and, in the process, restoring spiritual practices related to foods, while strengthening community health and self-determination" (191). Ultimately, as LaDuke explains, "the recovery of the people is tied to the recovery of food" (210), for food plays an essential role in the spiritual, physiological, historical, and environmental wellbeing of Native American life and culture.

Decolonial food activism also recognizes the way food acts as a vehicle for expressing and understanding ethnic identity. For Ronda L. Brulotte and Michael Di Giovine, food functions "as a marker of heritage [that] creates and reinforces ethnic group identity in an increasingly multicultural milieu" (3). The cultural meanings of food in America, however, cannot be understood apart from its colonial history. As Michael W. Twitty argues, contemporary Southern cuisine bears the imprint of various cultural exchanges rooted in colonial settlements, the slave trade, and Manifest Destiny: "All of the negotiations and conflict—between European indentures, Africans and Native people, with one another, and within their own groupings—affected how the food came to be and what we think of as soul or Southern" (163). These intersections between African American and Native American cultures offer one example of the way colonialism manifested itself in food. "Africans certainly influenced the food culture of Southern Natives, just as many of the basic building blocks of Southern food owed a direct link to Native ingenuity" (204), Twitty writes. This blending of different cuisines—like the erasure of Indigenous culinary traditions—reflects the legacy of colonial oppression, pointing to ethnic hierarchies that have empowered whites at the expense of Native Americans and African Americans. By uncovering these origins, the Indigenous food movement offers a powerful means for people to mitigate these injustices and to understand, celebrate, and embrace their cultural identity.

The complex meanings of food have become part of contemporary theater's exploration of identity as well.[4] According to Dorothy Chansky and Ann Folino White in *Food and Theatre on the World Stage,* food has established a new theatrical presence since the start of the twenty-first century, becoming "the very raison d'être for a complement of productions arising in the midst of an upswing in food politics and the ubiquity of food programming on television" (6). The centrality of food in such drama certainly speaks to its importance in our lives and in the way we understand others. It also speaks to the power that plays—like *August: Osage County*—have to help us recognize the social, cultural, economic, and environmental significance of what we eat. In Letts's work in particular, food becomes a means for interrogating the history of colonialism from the Trail of Tears to modern-day reservation life. It functions as a source of Johnna's moral authority while highlighting stereotypes that suppress Indigenous voices. And it condemns the environmental harm caused by modern food production.

Farming, Poverty, and Native American Culture

Letts has discussed the importance of Oklahoma history and Native American culture in the writing of *August: Osage County:* "If you're from Oklahoma, Native American life is part of your experience growing up. I myself am part Native American . . . My grandfather was born in Native American territory before it became a state . . . I always felt that inherent in the work was the idea that, perhaps, we have sown the seeds of our own destruction, by that genocide. And that Oklahoma, positioned right in the center of the country, was somewhat representative of a national shame."[5] Indeed, this setting embodies the violent legacy of colonial expansion in the United States. The coerced removal of Native Americans began in earnest in the nineteenth century. The War of 1812, for instance, provided Andrew Jackson with an opportunity to intensify his ruthless military campaign against Native Americans, and he negotiated numerous treaties that exchanged eastern territories for land in the West. Not long after defeating John Quincy Adams for the presidency, Jackson also pushed through Congress the Indian Removal Act of 1830, which essentially mandated the westward migration of all tribes.

These efforts were rooted, in part, in racist ideology. According to Alfred Cave, Jackson grounded the Indian removal policy in "his unquestioned belief in inherent Indian intellectual and moral inferiority" (135). He wanted, as J. M. Opal notes, "to turn southeastern North America into a vast domain of 'wealthy inhabitants unmixed by Indians,' a U.S. frontier rather than a multinational borderland" (156). Since Jackson viewed Native Americans as impediments to the economic progress of white farmers and plantation owners (including himself), he vowed as President to protect "white households" from having "to fear Indian country, or to get around it while rushing cash crops to foreign markets" (208). By the end of his second term, the Five Civilized Tribes "had ceded over 100 million acres of eastern land to the federal government in return for $68 million and 20 million acres of far less hospitable land west of the Mississippi" (Wickett 5). Forced removals continued in subsequent administrations, and by the 1850s, the government established the reservation system to facilitate them, offering payments and other incentives for relocation.

Oklahoma itself marked the end point for the infamous Trail of Tears, a forced migration that killed thousands of Native Americans, including at least six thousand Choctaws and four thousand Cherokees (Cave 154; Wickett 4). One of the relocated tribes, the Osage, had to relinquish their eastern territories in a series of legal agreements beginning in 1808 (Rollings 13). As a result of the Drum Creek Treaty in 1870, for instance, the U.S. government purchased the Osages' remaining lands in Kansas, and this sale enabled the tribe to buy and govern its own territory in Oklahoma. Such sovereignty would not last long, however. After decades of encroachment on the Osage Nation by white settlers and rival tribes, the United States annexed the territory in 1907 to form the state of Oklahoma. This loss of land and autonomy did not stop efforts to eradicate Native American culture through assimilation. According to Murray Wickett, politicians and white humanitarians used a "multi-pronged policy [that] embraced economic, educational, judicial, political, and social reform" (206). They "proposed to eliminate the 'Indian problem' by eliminating the Indians as a culturally distinct entity," and these efforts at erasure reflected the ongoing colonial mindset of the United States toward Native Americans. As Wickett concludes, "whites proved willing to accept Indians only when they in fact ceased to be Indians" (207).

Letts uses the Youngbirds' relationship with food as a tool for examining this history of Native American exploitation. In the prologue, Beverly shares his memory of Johnna's father: "I knew Mr. Youngbird . . . Small town. Bought many a watermelon from his fruit stand. Some summers he sold fireworks too, right? . . . I bought Roman candles for my children" (11–12). If Mr. Youngbird's ability to sustain his family and customers by cultivating food suggests a symbiotic relationship with the land, his life as a farmer nevertheless evokes American colonial history. The United States government established Oklahoma reservations, in part, to train the Plains tribes to abandon nomadic culture, and it provided agricultural tools, food rations, and instructors ("Indian agents") to teach them to become self-sufficient farmers. As Wickett notes, "officials concluded that they could only become civilized when they abandoned the nomadic lifestyle of the buffalo chase. Reformers felt that the reservation could serve as a laboratory in which the 'savages' could be transformed into civilized beings under the paternal care and guidance of local Indian agents" (94–95). Most of these agents were unable to help produce thriving farms, however, and they attributed this failure either to the inherent laziness of Native Americans or to the government's willingness to provide food rations. More than a hundred years later, Mr. Youngbird's "success" as a farmer has proven to be another form of oppression. Embracing an agricultural life, like anglicizing his name, has done nothing for him financially or socially.

Mr. Youngbird's fruit stand also reflects the limited economic opportunities associated with reservation life. Heat operates as the most prominent metaphor for this oppression in the play. When Barbara discusses the weather, she gazes at the Oklahoma landscape: "What were these people thinking? . . . The jokers who settled this place. The Germans and the Dutch and the Irish. Who was the asshole who saw this flat hot nothing and planted his flag? I mean, we fucked the Indians for *this*?" (25). Like other observations about the heat, these comments allude to the difficulties of working the land and of a colonial history that determined ownership for some at the expense of others. Such harsh conditions still exist for Mr. Youngbird, whose job requires laboring in the oppressive heat on land he does not own. He works himself to death, ultimately having a heart attack and falling "into a flatbed truck full of wine grapes" (12). This detail makes clear that Mr. Youngbird never earned enough money to stop being a laborer. His death—like the three parakeets that die from the heat inside Violet's house—also points to the dwindling population of Native Americans. According to Bigsby, "the Osage Reservation in Oklahoma [registered] a population of 156 in the 2010 census" (109), and American Indians made up only 14.7 percent of the population in Osage County in 2018 ("Quick Facts").

Mr. Youngbird not only dies while working, but he also cannot provide a more economically secure future for his daughter. Her aspirations to be a nurse are cut short by his death and the needs of her family: "I had to drop out [of Tulsa Community College] when Daddy died. And I saw my mom and grandma through bad times" (14). Just as Johnna cannot afford even the meager tuition of community college, her mother and grandmother cannot afford a caregiver, so they rely on their twenty-six-year-old daughter for help. This family offers a glimpse into a cycle of poverty that has trapped many Native Americans. Johnna's relationship with the Westons is no different than her father's. She works for them, relying on their money for survival, and this power dynamic highlights some of the socioeconomic hierarchies that have disenfranchised Native Americans. Whites can buy fireworks from Mr. Youngbird to celebrate the Fourth of July—a holiday marking the independence of a nation that has repeatedly and ruthlessly denied freedoms to Indigenous populations. Beverly can make the decision to kill himself. His work—even his presence—is not necessary for the survival of his wife and grown children. And he can hire Johnna to do the emotional and physical labor of family instead. The Westons are sustained, in other words, by the stagnation of people who have few options apart from working for them.

Finally, the fruit stand links Mr. Youngbird with a dying institution in the United States—that of the independent farmer. As Paul Roberts notes in *The End of Food*, "In 1885, more than half of the U.S. population was engaged in farming; in 1985, that share had fallen to less than 3 percent" (23). This dramatic shift can be attributed to the consolidation of the U.S. farm system by food companies and the rise of a high-volume, low-cost food model in the 1980s. This model transformed food into a commodity that necessitated the use of chemicals, preservatives, and artificial flavorings to enhance shelf life and to maximize corporate profits. The artificiality of processed foods—the majority of foods available in supermarkets, for instance—offers a reminder of the differences between the Youngbirds and the Westons. Members of the former family have a direct, natural relationship with what they eat. Members of the latter family are content with "cheese and saltines, or a ham sandwich" (31). The Westons must hire someone to cook, and they express no interest in the way food gets altered from farm to market. Their disconnection indicates a larger failing. It reveals the Westons—and middle-class America more broadly—to be not only victims of the marketplace but also increasingly dependent on the labor and skills of others for survival.

Cooking, Community, and Morality

The disconnectedness of the Weston family is also captured by Johnna's role as chef—particularly the way her cooking provides stability and even moral guidance. The family marvels at the quality and scope of her meals: "Johnna cooked this whole meal by herself" (65); "Johnna did it all" (64). The pronoun "it" hints at the larger significance of her actions. Johnna, in fact, feeds, nurtures, and protects them. Her food provides cohesion. It draws the family together—whether explicitly ("Come with me to the kitchen, let's see what it is" [21]) or metaphorically (through Mattie Fae's expression "give me some sugar" [26]). It provides comfort: "Kind of nice, huh?" (31). And it offers an invaluable way to diffuse tension. When Violet talks about selling the furniture to her daughters or insults Karen's impending marriage, for example, Steve, Karen, Ivy, Charles, and Barbara interject with compliments about dinner. Their repeated praise also suggests that shared meals and good food have been long absent from the Weston family. Just as Violet and Beverly care little about eating ("We don't eat. [. . .] I can't tell you the last time that stove, oh . . . turned on. Years" [31]), Mattie Fae's "inedible" casserole is a source of dread among the family (48). The horrors of the Westons' cooking are made clear when Little Charles leaves the casserole "for an hour inside a hot car" (60) and later drops the dish, which *lands with a sickening 'splat' on the dining room floor* (63). Ultimately, the lack of eating and failures in cooking underscore the absence of nurturing and community in the family home. The dinner devolves into a brawl. Food and furniture get knocked to the floor. And the disassembling of this meal reflects the fragmentation of the Weston family and the middle-class values that they represent.

Johnna's meals juxtapose the historical pressure to assimilate with myths about American progress as well. Johnna does not cook traditional Cheyenne cuisine. Instead, she makes food that will appeal to the Westons—traditional American dishes such as chicken and fried potatoes. Barbara proclaims, "she makes the best goddamn apple pie I ever ate in my life" (31), and Steve and Karen echo this sentiment after the funeral: "The food is just spectacular" (65). Such meals offer one sign of culinary injustice in the play. Though she partakes in each meal at the Weston house, suggesting a partial loss of her own cultural traditions, Johnna makes conscious efforts to celebrate her heritage in other ways, such as wearing her dried umbilical cord in a pouch around her neck and changing her name to "Monveta," the word for "young bird" in Cheyenne. Only Violet recognizes the contrast between Johnna's productivity and the Westons' inertia. At the funeral dinner, she announces Johnna's status as a domestic servant ("'Swhat she's paid for . . . You all did know she's getting paid, right?" [65]), in part, to link the hierarchy in the house with some of the socio-economic hierarchies that have left Johnna at the bottom. Not surprisingly, her presence prods Violet into attacking her children's limited accomplishments: "Where'd *you* wind up? (*Jabs a finger at Karen.*) Whadda *you* do? (*Jabs a finger at Ivy.*) Whadda *you* do? (*Jabs a finger at Barbara.*) Who're *you*? Jesus, you worked as hard as us, you'd all be president. You never had problems so you got to make all your problems yourselves" (71). Her diatribe reflects fears about the decline of her own family and white middle-class America more broadly. As Courtney Elkin Mohler notes, "the white characters . . . talk and scream constantly throughout the course of the epic play, but *do* almost nothing. Johnna's industry and skill illustrate a central aspect of the crisis of the white American middle class in the 2000s: lack of productivity" (139).

Confronted by this crisis, Violet uses Johnna's ethnicity to diminish her. Violet repeatedly mocks the notion that Johnna should be referred to as "Native American": "*Who* calls them that? Who *makes* that decision?" (31). When

Karen later expresses nostalgia for the childhood game of Cowboys and Indians, Violent corrects her: "Don't you know not to say 'Cowboys and Indians'? You played Cowboys and Native Americans" (68). Just as the game alludes to the violent conquest of the West, it also functions as a reminder that American culture has perpetuated stereotypes about Indigenous peoples as savage and primitive. Even Barbara's debate over terminology and her observations about genocide do not reflect any meaningful concern with this history of racial violence. She merely assumes Beverly's role as patriarch and employer in Act III, sitting at his desk, paying Johnna's salary, and praising her ability to lie about Beverly's fatherly affection ("That makes me feel better. Knowing that you can lie" [92]). Of course, Barbara's comfort with deception reflects a broader national investment in cultural myths that obfuscate the truth about racial and economic inequity. In this way, *August: Osage County* presents Violet's racism not as a manifestation of her drug addiction but as part of a long tradition of discrimination. Seeing Native American culture as unworthy of acknowledgement, she mirrors the attitude of the United States more generally. The play culminates with Johnna holding Violet like a child and singing the closing lines from T.S. Eliot's "The Hollow Men" (1925). The poem depicts the spiritual and cultural stagnation of the modern world along with the consequences of imperialism, as suggested by Eliot's epigraph from Joseph Conrad's *Heart of Darkness*. Eliot's desert space or "cactus land" (section 3, line 2) proves fitting for Oklahoma, and with this reference, Letts suggests that American dissipation can be attributed to the racist ideology that is used to justify its colonial history.

Johnna's moral grounding, along with her ability to cook, highlights another source of the Westons' decline. As Chansky notes in *Kitchen Sink Realisms*, the typical domestic figure onstage "is often fully able to get the job done while also handling emotional and political problems—sometimes including the problem of finding a way for the next generation to be able to focus on emotional and political problems without having to expend energy on housework" (9). Johnna certainly creates a relatively stable environment for them, greeting Barbara warmly ("Welcome home" [28]) and holding her after the news about Beverly's death (*"Johnna wraps one hand around Barbara's middle, places the other hand firmly on Barbara's forehead"* [41]). Without being asked, Johnna makes coffee for the family when the Sheriff wakes them with the tragic news. Food—from coffee to the apple pie that the Westons snack on throughout the play—enables the family's emotional work. The estranged siblings and Violet talk with one another, for instance, and Charlie finds the courage to defend his son against Mattie Fae's insults. At the same time, Letts presents Johnna as shouldering the moral and emotional load. Most notably, she uses a kitchen skillet to brain Steve when he tries to molest Jean: *"He reaches for the skillet.*

She swings again and smacks his knuckles . . . She wades in with a strong swing and connects squarely with his forehead. Steve goes down" (87). As she explains, "He was messing with Jean. So I tuned him up . . . He was kissing her and grabbing her" (87). This fearless assault stems from her clear sense of right and wrong, and though she uses a weapon emblematic of her role as cook, she also plays a maternal role, protecting Jean even at the risk of losing her job.

By contrast, the way Uncle Charlie says grace during the funeral dinner captures the Westons' failure to protect each other and their children: "We are truly blessed in our, our fellowship, our togetherness, our . . . our fellowship. Thank thee for the food, O Lord, that we can share this food and replenish our bodies with . . . with nourishment" (64). The stumbling language and repetition signal both the infrequency of prayer within the family and his struggles to say something positive. The pause before "with nourishment" captures his trouble articulating the emotional, spiritual, and moral desperation of the family. They need to "be better people" (64), but as this awkward grace illustrates, the Westons have no spiritual or cultural traditions to ground them. Unlike Johnna, who finds strength in her familial and cultural identity, the Westons are coming apart at the seams as evidenced through divorced spouses, estranged siblings, alienated children, negligent parents, and a dead father. Bill and Barbara worry about Jean's wellbeing, but only Johnna acts decisively in her defense. Though Barbara stays with Violet briefly after the family departs, only Johnna takes up residence in the house. While no one can stomach Mattie Fae's casserole, Johnna provides nourishing, delicious food. And she offers intimacy for characters who feel unloved and untouched.

Positioning Johnna as a source for moral authority, however, Letts also captures the challenges of overcoming racist ideology in white America. Johnna may assert her desire to work for the Westons in terms of personal agency and financial exigency: "I don't do it for you . . . I do it for me . . . I need the work" (91, 92). Yet Barbara sees no connection between this economic narrative and ethnic identity. Just as she fails to realize that the term "Native American" erases the cultural differences among tribes, she does not recognize the way whiteness enables a socioeconomic mobility denied to Johnna. Instead, Barbara uses this moment in the play to assert her own significance, framing their conversation with *"I'm* still here, goddam it" (92). She effectively replaces Johnna's story with her own, and in this way she highlights another dimension of the colonial mindset, one expressed in many places from the trope of the noble savage to contemporary representations of Indigenous characters as foils for white narratives. Cultural and culinary injustice stem from racist hierarchies that shape social practices and ways of thinking. Johnna operates as an agent of resistance against colonial injustice, whether by changing her name or striking Steve with a pan. But she is also used as a vehicle to focus the audience's attention on whiteness. She becomes, in other words, a reminder of white America's failure to view Native Americans as sufficient to serve as the center of their own stories.

Beef, Vegetarianism, and Environmental Harm

The specter of meat production adds a compelling dimension to *August: Osage County*, offering another example of the kind of exploitation that shapes and drives American culture. Before the funeral dinner, Steve tells Jean that he worked in the meatpacking industry: "You know what I was doing when I was fifteen . . . Cattle processing. You know what that is? . . . Slaughterhouse. Sanitation. Slaughterhouse sanitation . . . I don't recommend it. But hey. Put food on the table. Get it?" (54). Steve has witnessed the bloodiest, filthiest, and most violent aspects of food production in America—workings that remain (along with the dangers of eating so much meat) hidden to most consumers.[6] Steve's experiences do not alter his eating habits, however, and his appetite for meat becomes a metaphor for his unchecked carnal hungers. His salacious desire for Jean, for example, is signaled initially through word play about getting "fucked up" together, and Jean's insistence that Steve smells "food, from the kitchen," not marijuana on her, equates her with meat, with something to consume (54). His appetite for the flesh—in this case for Jean—give some insight into his three divorces as well as his unethical business practices. Steve's actual job, which he describes as "security work," remains obscure. Apparently, he hides money from the Middle East in offshore accounts, and these shady practices prompt Bill to label his job as mercenary. Steve's response—"I think of it more like 'missionary' than 'mercenary'" (53)—resonates with Letts's larger critique of colonialism. Whether motivated by the greedy acquisition of land and goods, religious conversion, or cultural assimilation, colonialism is inherently about exploitation. Steve embodies this impulse here, equating meat-eating with lust for women, and profiting from a region where two U.S. wars, in Iraq and Afghanistan, were ongoing at the time the play was written.

Jean has a different attitude toward food, and her vegetarianism further underscores the moral failings of the Westons. When asked about her aversion to meat, Jean explains: "When you eat meat, you ingest an animal's fear . . . I mean even if you don't sort of think of it spiritually, what happens to *you*, when you feel afraid? . . . Your body goes through this whole chemical process when it experiences fear . . . So when you eat an animal, you're eating all that fear it felt when it was slaughtered to make food" (66). On one hand, her sentiments allude to the way the meatpacking industry alters meat through antibiotics, ammonia, and other chemicals. On the other hand, her view aligns with the Hindu and Buddhist philosophy of nonviolence to all living creatures. Yet it is not surprising that Jean makes her argument outside the context of spirituality, for the Westons do not appear deeply invested in any religious traditions. Nor does she discuss the environmental benefits of eating less meat. None of the Westons express an interest in protecting the land or preserving natural resources. Like the colonial history behind culinary erasure in the United States, the meatpacking industry has wiped out or consolidated most independent cattle and chicken farmers in the service of mass production. The consequences of these efforts—from the inhumane treatment of animals to severe environmental harm—remain unacknowledged by the Westons.

Needless to say, Jean's vegetarianism becomes a target of mockery during dinner, but the family's comments about meat reinforce the way Letts crafts their dissipation as emblematic of a national decline. Most of the humor functions like the compliments about Johnna's cooking—as a tool for deflecting Violet's ire—yet it also allows Letts to poke fun at American excesses. Charlie, for example, consumes meat with every meal: "God, you mean I've been eating fear, what, three times a day for sixty years! . . . I guess it was the way I was raised, but it just doesn't seem like a legitimate meal unless it has some meat somewhere" (66). His addiction to meat—emblematic of national appetites—stems in part from his upbringing, a detail that highlights consumption as a learned behavior. It passes along its consuming and consumerist ethos from generation to generation. When he later jokes that "fear never tasted so good," Barbara ribs her daughter as well: "I catch her eating a cheeseburger every now and again . . . Double cheeseburger with bacon, extra fear" (68). The joke implies that Barbara considers Jean's newfound vegetarianism a phase, and Barbara knows from her lifelong experiences that responsible behavior does not last long in the Weston family. Jean, meanwhile, has cast her argument against meat-eating not in moral or social terms but instead in terms of its impact on the self. However, selfishness is central to the problem with both the Westons in particular and American culture more broadly. Throughout its history of colonial expansion and tireless consumption of natural resources, the nation has subjugated nonwhites for the social and economic benefit of whites. It has devoured natural resources at an unsustainable rate to buttress a consumer marketplace. And all of these failings have cultural, moral, and environmental implications.

Finally, when Violet references fast food, this moment reinforces the link between food and cultural decline in the play. After Charlie declares that legitimate meals must have meat, Mattie Fae adds, "If I make a pasta dish of some kind, he'll just be like, 'Okay, that was good for an appetizer, now where's the meat?'" (66). Violet then tries to recall the famous 1984 Wendy's slogan,

"Where's the beef?" and though one daughter corrects her, Violet begins screeching: "*'Where's the meat?!' 'Where's the meat?!' 'Where's the meat?'*" The substitution of "meat" for "beef" is a reaction to the family's repeated attempts to derail her from "truth-telling." She wants to discuss something more substantive, something meatier, and her preferred "truths" include humiliating memories of Beverly, personal insults, a proprietary claim to the inheritance, and anecdotes about her family's past hardships on the Plains. For Violet, the truth of the Westons is one of loss—the loss of familial connections, intimacy, and grit. The allusion to fast food underscores this message. Prepared outside the home with cheap ingredients, fast food is made and consumed quickly, even thoughtlessly, and its prominent role in American culture suggests a breakdown of the traditions associated with family and community.

Food, Compassion, and Healing

In discussing the premiere production of *August: Osage County,* Letts recalls, "The actress who originated the role [of Johnna], an Oklahoma native named Kim Guerrero, was Cherokee. And she said to us while we were rehearsing that the idea she had been raised with, by other natives, was that, 'This is our land, the white people are here for a while using it, we're going to be good to them while they're here, and then when they're gone it's going to be our land again.' That was kind of a governing principle when I was writing the piece."[7]

The tension between ownership and compassion emerges as a central theme in the play, and Letts places Mr. Youngbird and Johnna at the center of this tension. Both characters have been victimized by the history of American colonialism. They have lost access to their culinary tradition. They possess neither land nor enough money to attend college. Instead, they remain locked in a cycle of poverty that requires them to work for the descendants of the settlers who benefited from Native American relocation and the reservation system. Their relationship with food provides a powerful reminder of this exploitation. Mr. Youngbird works himself to death as a farmer. Johnna abandons her studies as a nurse to cook for the Westons.

As caretakers, both father and daughter highlight the lack of caring in the Weston house. Beverly and Violet's disinterest in eating, for example, reflects their indifference to each other; food has been replaced by alcohol and pills to cope with their feelings of resentment and guilt. Mattie Fae's inability to cook represents her failings as a wife, sister, and mother. And Jean tries to distinguish herself from the rest of the family by not eating meat. It comes as little surprise that the Westons need to hire someone to cook and clean because none of them appear invested in the work of family. They may be landowners, employers, and educators. They may be historical beneficiaries of racist exploitation and marginalization in the United States, yet they appear stuck—in relationships broken by deception and in families diminished by an absence of tradition and spiritual grounding.

In these ways, Letts positions the Westons as representative of an American middle class that has been stained by the nation's history and lost something as a result. Amid the turmoil, alienation, and hungers of modern life, the Westons do not turn to each other but to Johnna for help. She provides a counter-model for identity rooted in tradition and family. Wearing her umbilical cord in the pendant around her neck and reverting to her Cheyenne name, Johnna holds on to traditions not already lost to her. She may be able to cook only white American cuisine, but her skills as a chef—like her father's career as a farmer—reveal her family's ability to nurture others and the land. Ultimately, Johnna's cultural traditions and relationship to the land offer the greatest indictment of American colonial history. They not only draw attention to a lack within the Weston family, but they also comment on America's insatiable appetites. These hungers have fueled the exploitation of nonwhite people and nature itself, particularly in regard to food production. And they continue to influence the social prejudices and economic limitations that are the legacy of colonialism and that try to erase cultural differences. In the context of the play, the Westons cannot get enough meat (when they eat at all), and Native Americans—whether through their physical labor or their stereotypical representations—still appear to be an exploitable resource.

CHAPTER 5

Mary Page Marlowe and the
Patchwork of Personal Identity

After the death of his mother in 2014, Tracy Letts began writing *Mary Page Marlowe*—a play about personal identity and womanhood in America. This "internal examination . . . of what makes a person a person" operates, to some extent, as an invitation for self-reflection. "That is part of what we do hopefully, ideally, in the theatre," Letts explains. "We give people an opportunity to look at themselves, and I think in the case of *Mary Page Marlowe*, we give them the opportunity to look at themselves with love and forgiveness."[1] By inviting audiences to identify with Mary, Letts also forces them to confront the challenges of being a woman in a patriarchal society. Mary laments the various roles expected of her (daughter, lover, wife, mother) because they come at the expense of her own freedom. Yet she refuses to be defined by any one aspect of her life. Mary struggles for self-understanding and, in the process, reveals a strength and complexity common in Letts's oeuvre—from gun-toting Dottie Smith to the indomitable Violet Weston. As Letts admits, such women have "always fascinated me, mystified me, aggravated me, enticed me, terrified me. I suppose it comes as a result of having a lot of good, smart, strong women in my life. They seem to be—I'm going to get myself in trouble—the superior gender. Maybe that's why they've gotten a raw deal."[2] Indeed, Mary encounters gender hierarchies throughout her life that confound and compromise her identity, and she must overcome these "raw deals" to know herself.

Spanning nearly seventy years, *Mary Page Marlowe* traces the titular protagonist through infancy, childhood, college, fraught marriages, incarceration, and a hospital visit shortly before her death. Each scene gives a momentary glimpse into her life while highlighting the way gender circumscribes her aspirations and choices. The play opens with forty-year-old Mary explaining the custody arrangement of her divorce to her children, Wendy and Louis. The next scene jumps to a tarot card reading in college that reveals her view of marriage as antithetical to freedom, particularly her dream of traveling to Paris. This moment is followed by sixty-three-year-old Mary and her third husband learning that she has completed the terms of her parole, but this news ultimately underscores the absence of female friendships in her life. In Scene Four, ten-month-old Mary fusses in a crib while her parents fight. The next glimpse, set in a psychiatrist's office, details her extramarital affairs, which are motivated by a desire to have something separate from marriage and motherhood. Scene Six places Mary in the hospital close to her death as she reflects on the mistakes in her life. One of these mistakes gets depicted in the following scene when she decides to plead guilty for nearly killing a man while driving drunk—an act of personal responsibility that begins the dissolution of her second marriage. The eighth scene captures an extramarital affair with her boss in a motel room, and Scene Nine reveals the moment twelve-year-old Mary learns of her mother's plans to travel to California to find her ex-husband. Mary at the age of forty-four appears next, frantically looking for her son who has become a drug addict and a runaway. Her reliance on Wendy at this moment provides an opportunity to praise her daughter's strong sense of self.

The final scene of the play occurs at a dry cleaner with Mary asking about a family quilt that she recently found in storage. To some extent, Letts presents this quilt as an image both for Mary's fragmented sense of self and for the structure of the play—eleven scenes that offer glimpses into her life with no chronological order or resolution. According to Bigsby, Mary's life is "like a quilt in need of attention" (*Twenty-First*, 116), and the play itself, as Isherwood notes, "is stitched together haphazardly as the story unfolds, leaving us to fill in the gaps and to try to ferret out connections that Mr. Letts intends us to infer." These connections can best be understood, however, through the history of American quilting. Just as Mary stitches together personal experiences in an effort to understand herself, the audience assembles these panels to get a clearer picture of the challenges facing women in modern America. Quilts have played a crucial role in the personal, social, and artistic lives of women throughout much of U.S. history. Whether indicating elite social status or reflecting mainstream tastes, producing practical bed coverings or commemorating special events, quilts have provided important outlets for artistic expression and female community. Not surprisingly, the popularity of this craft has made its way into other arts such as literature, and even though some early feminists expressed reservations about quilting, contemporary scholars consider it an invaluable way to examine female identity, traditions, and modes of expression

throughout American history. Starting with a brief overview of American quilting and its place in women's literature, this chapter examines Letts's portrait
of patriarchal institutions that demand the appearance of domestic harmony
over emotional truth and pressure women into performing roles that provide
no room for female autonomy. Like Mary's open-ended narrative, which resists
closure and chronology, Letts ultimately makes her unfinished quilt an image
for the work that still needs to be done to achieve greater gender equality in
America.

Cultural Identity, Community, and Feminism in American Quilting

Quilting played an important role in the lives of girls and women in early
America. Diaries from the eighteenth and nineteenth centuries give detailed
accounts of stitching and patchwork, and the average American girl completed
her first quilt by the age of five. For the most part, these childhood efforts were
stitched in school settings with the help of a teacher, and this academic instruction focused on organizational principals that directly influenced the geo-
metric designs of needlework. Quilting continued into adolescence with young
women drawing inspiration from their daily lives as well as from British, European, African, and Native American cultures. According to Elaine Showalter,
most women typically had twelve quilts in their dowry chest before making a
Bridal Quilt—a painstaking expression of love, social status, and community.
This part of the trousseau tended to use "the most expensive materials the
family could afford," and its completion relied on the talents of both family
members and neighbors (148). Quilts from the seventeenth century through the
early 1800s, however, were not considered necessities but luxuries, primarily
used as decorative bedcovers by upper-class women. As Robert Shaw notes,
"fabric—especially printed cottons that were relatively easy to cut and sew and
therefore best suited to pieced and appliqué quiltmaking—was imported from
England, and it was expensive, putting it out of reach of all but the well-to-do"
(20). Such quilts also required the kind of time and assistance, through domestic help, found only in upper-class homes.

After the Civil War, quilting entered middle- and lower-class life thanks to
the technological innovations of the Second Industrial Revolution. The expansion of textile mills in New England and the South, for example, increased the
affordability and availability of fabrics. This coincided with the development
of the sewing machine, which made the process of quilting faster and easier.
In 1851 Isaac Singer patented a device with a straight—instead of curved—
needle that had up-and-down motion and moved in a straight line, enabling
an unprecedented 900 stitches per minute. After modifying the design to use
interchangeable parts, which lowered the cost, Singer introduced a three-year

payment plan, and the home sewing machine soon became a mainstay in American households. By 1871, 700,000 machines were being manufactured annually (Shaw 123). Women's magazines, which grew in popularity at this time, helped fuel a national quilting craze, promoting a range of needlework fads. Businesses quickly capitalized on this trend by selling instruction manuals, templates, sample patterns, and other quiltmaking aids (Hanson 1). Quilts also started to become more versatile. Instead of being used merely as bedcovers, they commemorated important events, honored the dead, expressed patriotism, and even commented on war. According to Deborah Deacon, women's textiles served "as historical records, as inspirations in battle such as banners and flags, as commemorations and remembrances, and as expressions of the impacts of war on themselves and their families" (44). This versatility—along with intricate designs now possible through sewing machines—encouraged women to expand the artistic possibilities of quilting for individual and communal expression.

The technological innovations at the turn of the century inspired a great deal of anxiety as well, and quilting became one outlet for these concerns. At the end of the 1800s, for example, two artistic movements emerged that commented directly on the social changes brought on by modern technology. According to Marin Hanson, "both the Aesthetic Movement, dominant during the 1870s and 1880s, and the Colonial Revival, strongest from the 1890s through the 1930s, shared anti-industrial, anti-modern roots and attempted to answer the question of how to mitigate the negative impact of industrialization on society" (2). The Aesthetic Movement viewed the modern era—with its proliferation of factories, coal-fueled machinery, labor unrest, and urban areas—as making the landscape uglier. It celebrated "art for art's sake," and this mantra soon found application in the decorative arts. Specifically, the beautification of the home, practitioners argued, had the ability to transport the occupant to a time before industrialization. One notable example of this trend, the Crazy Quilt, was inspired by Japanese designs first introduced to U.S. audiences in World's Fairs. It featured jarring contrasts in patterns, designs, textures, and materials along with elaborate embroidery. Such decorative objects, called fancywork, endowed the home with both aesthetic and moral character. "Not only did fancywork make the home more pleasant," as Hanson argues, "but it had the appeal of being handmade, not manufactured by a lifeless machine" (3).

Unlike the British origins of the Aesthetic Movement, the Colonial Revival was distinctly American, expressing an anti-modern sentiment through its idealization of the nation's colonial past. This vision of the country's origins had little to do with the realities of the colonial era. Instead, it imagined the nation's ancestors as simple, industrious, and morally grounded. In fact, the

Colonial Revival enabled women to use quilts as a means to connect themselves with history. As Cynthia Prescott argues, "placing quilts in Colonial-style rooms also put the women who made them into the story of history. American women began to shape the interpretation of Colonial Revival, using quilts as a powerful strategy" (231). Needlework thus became a gateway for women to learn more about their own familial and national roots and to insert themselves into these narratives. Through these efforts, women "found themselves wanting to know more about the earlier women who had made quilts and textiles" (233), and their work came to represent the importance of women's place in American history.

Finally, quilting also provides a history of female community in the United States. Quilting bees—social gatherings that marked important events such as engagements, marriages, births, and deaths—not only offered opportunities for women to share their artistic skills but also to socialize, forge friendships, discuss politics, and exchange personal stories. As Shaw and others have noted, few quilts were created at these events per se. Individuals did most of the work, but women often relied on bees for the stitching process—"the most time-consuming part of making a quilt and therefore a prime candidate for community support" (Shaw 91). In some cases, the style of quilt lent itself to collaboration. The use of block patterns, for instance, inspired the friendship quilt in which "blocks were made by different women, and were typically inscribed with names, quotations, or other texts" (Gordon and Horton 94–5). Bees also encouraged exchanges between young and old. Rural mothers taught their daughters to sew, and it was not uncommon for women in the nineteenth century to continue sewing into their fifties and sixties. As Aimee E. Newell explains, older women found value in needlework as they sought to share their experiences with younger generations and to express nostalgia for the past: "Aging women had their own experiences that affected their work: changes in their bodies and minds; an increasing nostalgia for the past; and memories to reflect on and remember, which were portrayed in their quilts and samplers" (182). Whether motivated by a shared communal event, farming, politics, religion, war, or nostalgia, quilting was a distinctly female art form that allowed women to tell their stories, to share their lives, and to weave their experiences into that of American history. It was a practical art that offered comfort and warmth. And it gave one a sense of belonging to a family or community.

Within the literary and dramatic arts, quilting has often been used to comment on women's lives. Nineteenth-century writers such as Lydia Marie Child, Harriet Beecher Stowe, and Louisa May Alcott, for example, considered piecing emblematic of women's experiences—whether weaving together fragments of household fabrics in their spare time or working on a quilt with others (Witzling 629). Even though the quilt has continued to be used as a literary device in the twentieth and twenty-first centuries, it was a source of contention among early feminists. Female-centered arts were typically perceived as frivolous in the 1800s, and many feminists feared these literary applications would discredit women writers. By the 1880s, the temperance movement started associating quilts with an older generation, and many New Women and suffragists viewed them as symbols for female subjection. This rejection continued into the first half of the twentieth century. As Showalter notes, many women writers "scorned needlework metaphors in an effort to dissociate their work from the insulting imputations of feminine triviality" (161). Only with the second wave of feminism in the 1960s and 1970s did a reevaluation occur, and quilt studies, which aligns women's cultural history with the development of textiles in America, emerged.

Most notably, second-wave feminism celebrated the quilt's fragmented, decentered quality, its relationship to female community, and its ability to pass down stories from generation to generation. As historian Mara Witzling notes, quilting "is a medium that has enabled, and continues to enable, women to create works in which they speak the truth about their lives" (619). The importance of this practice has been celebrated in contemporary fiction. For black feminist writers in particular, quilts have offered invaluable insight into African American women's history and traditions that would otherwise be lost. Alice Walker, for example, uses them as a window into the legacy of slavery in *The Color Purple* (1982) and "Everyday Use" (1973), and even her approach to writing has been compared to quilt making. As critic Barbara Christian explains, the author "creates out of seemingly disparate everyday materials patterns of clarity, imagination, and beauty" (461). Other African American writers use quilts in their examination of black history, including Toni Morrison and Phyllis Alesia Perry.[3] More recently, the works of Zora Neale Hurston have inspired quilting exhibits in South Carolina in 2010 and Alabama in 2019.[4] In the context of the second wave of feminism and as these more recent examples suggest, the quilt holds a particularly important place among black female artists. Of course, quilting imagery appears in other ethnic literatures, and both men and women integrate it into their writings. From John Steinbeck to Margaret Atwood, Dorothy Parker to Toni Morrison, Leslie Marmon Silko to Sherman Alexie, and Susan Glaspell to Tracy Letts, the quilt emerges as a powerful image for lost women's voices and the importance of female community. It points to traditions—cultural and social—that have shaped women's lives. And it provides a reminder of social, economic, and racial hierarchies that have oppressed women.

Community and Female Identity in *Mary Page Marlowe*

In the summer of 1916, Susan Glaspell's *Trifles* premiered in a small theater on a wharf in Provincetown, Massachusetts, and it has remained one of the masterpieces of the Provincetown Players—a group of Greenwich Village artists that helped launch the little theater movement in New York. In this one-act play, two women piece together the motive for murder among the "trifles" of their neighbor Mrs. Wright. The erratic sewing of her log cabin quilt signals a breaking point in her marriage, and it leads the women to other clues that explain why she killed her husband. Yet the depth of Mrs. Wright's isolation and unhappiness, like the other evidence in the kitchen, goes unnoticed by the men in the play. The quilt not only reveals the truth about Mrs. Wright's psychological state, but it also becomes a text that forges a connection among these women. As Mrs. Hale laments, "I know how things can be—for women . . . We live close together and we live far apart. We all go through the same things—it's all just a different kind of the same thing." This sameness captures Glaspell's critique of the way men oppress, trivialize, and remain blind to the struggles of women.

One hundred years later, Tracy Letts's *Mary Page Marlowe,* which premiered at Steppenwolf Theatre Company in 2016, makes the quilt a central metaphor for understanding a woman's life as well.[5] In many ways, Letts evokes the history of American quilting to give Mary's story and her life the kind of significance she feels it lacks. The play's nonlinear structure and gaps present women's experiences as fragmented by patriarchal oppression. The challenge of piecing together this narrative, in other words, mirrors the pressure many women feel to negotiate personal identity relative to marriage and motherhood. More specifically, through Mary's failed attempts to use travel, sex, and alcohol to escape the oppressiveness of these roles, Letts captures the need among women for self-determination and self-expression. Mary's discovery of the family quilt at the end of the play provides the most powerful image for achieving this sense of autonomy. It places Mary's experiences in the broader context of women's lives in America. It celebrates female community and traditions. And it becomes a testament to the need for women to weave their own identities separately from men.

Mary's desire to travel becomes the first way the play explores the cost of sacrificing female community and selfhood for marriage. The glimpse of Mary's college life in Scene Two, for example, depicts three girls sharing their hopes about the future over a tarot deck. Just as Mary rejects a recent marriage proposal in favor of her freedom ("I don't want to be married. I just feel too independent for all that" [19].), her subsequent abortion indicates a similar attitude about motherhood. She rejects these roles because they would impede her "dreams and possibilities" (17). Nothing embodies this desire for freedom more than travel: "I hate it here [Ohio]. Wouldn't you like to see what else is out there? . . . I want to see Paris" (20). This choice, inspired by Audrey Hepburn's *Charade* (1963), equates Paris with some of the characteristics of the film. Hepburn's "Reggie" seeks a divorce from her thieving husband, and Cary Grant's character tries on numerous identities to disguise his work for the U.S. government. To some degree, Mary wants to find the right identity for herself even if it means rejecting marriage. Her choice to have a family, however, not only traps her in Ohio and Kentucky, but it also disconnects her from other women. Nowhere else in the play do we see Mary with female friends, and this distance is expressed most clearly when she tells her therapist that "I just found out my college girlfriend Lorna died from breast cancer last month" (34). For Letts, this moment highlights the dangers of positioning motherhood and marriage as antithetical to community. Women should not have to sacrifice the support network of other women to be attentive wives and nurturing mothers. Doing so can prove dangerous, as many of Mary's self-destructive choices illustrate. Her ultimate failing comes from quilting her story without the help of other women, and from disconnecting herself from the power their voices could have had to support her own.

The use of geography and travel in the opening scene also reinforces this message about marriage as a potential impediment for self-awareness. While sitting in a Denny's restaurant, Louis asks for help filling in a map of the United States: "I always get these mixed up" (7). Mary finds this confusion, particularly his inability to remember family trips, baffling: "You know this. 'Cause we've been there . . . You don't know where you've been?" (8). In many respects, this exchange encapsulates Mary's concerns about her own identity. As Letts indicates through the play's structure, there is no roadmap for self-understanding, and these assembled panels of memory highlight the way personal discovery does not unfold in straight lines or in logical steps. Mary does not reveal her own infidelities in this scene, the implicit cause of the divorce, nor does she explain the reason for losing her job, the likely result of an affair with a colleague or boss as suggested later. The detours and missteps of this journey signal her broader existential crisis with a culture that views motherhood and marriage as the only viable options for women. Like the sameness of Denny's and other chain restaurants, these limited possibilities capture the way many women feel pressured to follow a prescribed path. Perhaps it comes as little surprise that Mary never gets farther than Ohio and Kentucky. She never discovers the differences between Paris and Ohio, just as she never knows what it is like not to marry or to have children.

Her discussion in this scene about the custody arrangement for the divorce, which will require the children to move to Kentucky with her, makes the limited geography of her life an image for the forces that trap women as well. Wendy protests the move, begging to finish her last two years of high school in Ohio, but she learns that her father has rejected this possibility. As Mary explains, "He wants . . . he wants to keep you guys for the rest of the school year [. . .] He wants me to come up and stay with you on the weekends [. . .] He wants you [. . .] to live with me starting this summer" (10). The repetition of "he wants" privileges his desires here, placing the onus of childrearing primarily (and unquestioningly) on her. Later in the conversation, "he" gets replaced by "we" ("We agree this is the way to do this" [11]; "We thought" [12]), and though this moves Mary in the direction of self-expression, she cannot bring herself to speak in the first person about the divorce. In fact, Wendy's anger about moving is exacerbated by her mother's failure to express an opinion, and Letts communicates the feminist sensibility of the play, in part, through Wendy's string of questions: "What do you want? . . . Why can't you say what you want? . . . What about you, are you still Mary Page Gilbert, or do you go back to your old name?" Mary's silences and stilted responses suggest that marriage has compromised her voice to some degree. When she finally reclaims her maiden name, however, she begins the process of selfhood once again: "I haven't, I don't know. No, I'll go back to Marlowe" (13). This move from "he" to "we" to "I" captures the trajectory of Mary's lifelong struggles to be "Mary Page Marlowe" within the context of various roles that have often necessitated the loss of freedom. The choice to use her maiden name, like the act of stating her full name at the end of the play, presents individual identity as something women must fight to achieve.

Unable to travel, Mary turns to sex as a vehicle for self-expression, but these attempts to escape her roles as wife and mother only reinforce the extent of her entrapment: "My affairs . . . might be one area of my life where I could break out and just be the person I am without the playacting . . . But even there, I'm acting out a part, this easy girl, kind of dirty, won't make trouble" (36). Letts captures this dynamic explicitly in Scene Eight, offering a glimpse into Mary's affair with her boss several years earlier. After sex, Dan seeks reassurance about his desirability, in part, by reminding her of his power as her boss. Mary challenges the idea of this affair as obligating her in the future, but his discomfort with her control over their intimacy forces a performance of the "easy," "kind of dirty" lover: "I'm not saying we can't do it again. You get me very turned on. You're very handsome, and very sexy. You have a great, beautiful cock . . . Yeah, you turned on, baby?" (49, 50). The lines are intended to ring false, but Dan's pleasure underscores a discomforting truth about the pressure women feel to placate male desires. Mary's infidelities thus prove to be an ineffective means for moving beyond the inauthentic and for expressing something true about herself. Instead, she admits that "the only reason I've ever had sex is shame, guilt, power, attention" (36). This list, like the reasons missing from it such as personal pleasure, passion, desire, and even love, reveals some of the consequences of suppressing the self. Perhaps, it comes as little surprise that Mary claims not to be "the person I am. I'm just *acting* like a person who is a wife and a mother" (36). She has learned to cultivate the "right" appearances: "I know the levers to pull to be that person." When asked who is pulling the levers, however, Mary admits that she does not know. Yet her experiences suggest that cultural expectations privileging male power pull the levers. They deny women autonomy and visibility. They force them into roles that inspire humiliation and regret. And they pressure them to sacrifice a sense of self for the needs of others, never encouraging a way to balance the two.

Alcohol provides yet another failed outlet for coping with the demands of marriage and motherhood. While desperately trying to track down her drug-addicted son in Scene Ten, drinking fails to mitigate the costs of motherhood on Mary's identity. To some extent, Louis's history of substance abuse mirrors her self-destructive addiction to alcohol. She drinks throughout this scene even after Wendy pleads with her to stop, and as the audience learns in Scene Seven, Mary will go to jail six years later for a third DUI. Part of her frustration with Louis stems from the harmful impact of his addiction on her: "He needs some serious help because this is wearing me out. He has—you will find this out when you have kids of your own, it's unavoidable, but—he has *aged* me" (63). On one level, the assertion "it's unavoidable" positions suffering as inherent to motherhood, as if all women are aged by the experience of raising a child. On another level, this aside suggests the inevitability of Wendy having kids. Many women feel pressured to have children, and Mary assumes her daughter will follow the same path, with the same oppressive results. When Wendy describes her current romantic relationship as not having much of a future, however, Mary confesses admiration: "I respect you . . . I get mad at you sometimes because you seem inflexible, but the truth is: you are your own person . . . That's not easy, you know. For us" (65). To some extent, Wendy uses this moment to position herself as different from her mother. She does not drink. She refuses to date multiple men at the same time. And she does not seem concerned about finding a husband. Yet the phrase "for us" broadens the implications of their exchange by enabling Letts to make Mary representative of the struggles most women face to achieve personhood. She becomes a reminder of the challenges of balancing individual identity with one's relationships to children and spouses.

Mary's alcoholism, which leads to a car accident with serious legal rami-fications, does ultimately provide a path for her to come to terms with herself and to affirm her voice. At first, her husband Ray suggests that she plead not guilty because "a lot of guilty people don't go to prison" (42). Mary's deci-sion to accept responsibility for her actions, however, reflects a longing for self-acceptance: "I will pay this price, no matter how great, because it is what I must do. Because it is what I deserve. Because I am guilty" (46). This moment harkens back to the tarot reading at the beginning of the play: "You are in charge of your own destiny . . . Nothing is going to let you off the hook. You're responsible" (20). This advice immediately follows Mary's statement: "I'll be me." Personal responsibility, in other words, is an essential part of identity, and the fifty-year-old Mary in Scene Seven finally appears ready to accept herself. To reinforce this message, the New York production of *Mary Page Marlowe* in the summer of 2018 staged the Mary from each scene as lingering for a few moments to gaze at the Mary from the next. These acts of looking underscored this quest to see herself clearly, reinforcing Letts's message about identity and ownership. Mary repeats a variation of "this is the price I am going to pay" throughout this scene to lay claim to her life choices—including all of her fail-ings and limitations. Just as she refuses to look for a legal loophole or to lie about her guilt, she refuses to continue occupying prescribed roles that obfus-cate her identity.

Only by recognizing the use of alcohol as a coping mechanism for the literal and figurative losses in her life can Mary reclaim her voice. According to Ray, their marriage has been defined by this destructive addiction—from passing out at their wedding reception to blowing a point-three-two the night of the acci-dent. His references to "the unhappy marriages, the misery you and I have gone through, your tragedy" suggest that her alcohol abuse has, in part, been a tool to mitigate heartache (45). In addition to the death of her son ("your tragedy"), his observation about "unhappy marriages" foreshadows the dissolution of this one. Ray cannot accept his wife going to prison for two years, in part, because of the embarrassment of explaining "to everyone at work that my wife can't join me tonight because she's in a state prison . . . I'm a salesman, and you may not care about it, but things like appearances make a difference" (45). Mary's struggle with marriage once again involves the demand it places on women to perform certain roles, to privilege appearance over authenticity. Ray's condem-nation may involve Mary's refusal to be a salesman's wife any longer, but Letts makes clear that it also comes from a fundamental blindness about her identity. When he accuses her of "being out of touch with the way you feel about any-thing" (46), she *"explodes"* (per Letts's stage direction), and in the New York production, Mary (Kellie Overbey) slaps Ray twice at this moment: "You don't know anything about the way I feel! . . . Are we still screaming at each other?! Because I can scream! I've got a voice and I CAN SCREAM!" (46). It is, once again, the end of a marriage that enables her to reclaim her voice, and this anger comes from the way marriage has repeatedly caused her to mask her identity, to hide her emotions in order to perform various roles. Screaming seems to be the only way for her husband—and men more broadly—to hear a woman's needs.

Finally, Letts uses Mary's therapy session in Scene Five, which highlights her feelings of victimhood and inauthenticity, to provide the play's clearest critique of patriarchal oppression. Her victimization by marriage and mother-hood stems largely from the way these roles have robbed her of choice: "The truth is you and I pretend I make decisions about the direction of my life. I don't. I haven't . . . Like a migrating bird. I just did what seemed natural" (34). In some ways, Letts uses this imagery to point to the tension between the bio-logical and cultural forces that shape women's lives. Mary compares her move-ments to that of migrating birds, suggesting that her bodily drives directed her to motherhood, yet her frustration is not about this role per se but rather about the illusion that she had a choice about the outcome: "Why lose sleep over it if it's all just accidental? Someone else could have written my diary" (34). Inter-estingly, Mary's sense that she is not writing her own story shifts the biological narrative to a cultural one. Like the word "pretend," Mary's diary highlights her struggles to navigate between the genuine and inauthentic, the performa-tive and real, and Letts comments on the cultural bind facing women through this tension: "I just think as a woman, a lot of our roles get stipulated for us, and there's only one way to be a wife, a daughter, be a mom. Be a lover" (36). These expectations force women into social performances that sacrifice some-thing true about themselves for something artificial. Consequently, Mary views herself as "unexceptional," claiming that her diary can be written by anyone, because she feels no different than any other wife, mother, lover, and daughter.

Mary's Quilt and Female Identity

In the final scene of the play, Mary describes her family quilt to her dry cleaner, and Letts presents this image as an embodiment of women's art, of Mary her-self, and of the challenges facing female identity in American culture. She begins by explaining the collaborative nature of quilting: "Different women would sew the different panels and then stitch them all together . . . The women were not using all the same materials" (68). Like the play itself, this Colonial Revival quilt is comprised of different panels, different glimpses into the lives of the women in her family. The variety of materials speaks to the distinctiveness of each artist and of the various time periods ("generations") it represents. Letts also presents the quilt as a forgotten artifact to reinforce the play's message about the forces that silence and suppress female identity: "I was cleaning some stuff out of storage, trying to get some things together, when I came across it. I forgot I even had it, to tell you the truth" (69). Just as Mary has lost contact with her female friends from college, she has become disconnected from her own familial roots and, most notably, from the history of the women in her family. Her desire to restore and repair the quilt becomes a reminder of the importance of this community. It reflects an attempt to stitch her own story into the fabric of her family—to become part of a tradition that embraces female community and artistry.

In a deft touch, Letts makes Mary's favorite panel an image of obscured identity, encapsulating her lifelong struggles to achieve individuality: "The other panels show various frontier women, probably some of the women who started the work on it, farm women, and milkmaids, and baby girls, grandmothers in their shawls, that sort of thing. But this one panel shows a woman, in a long dark blue dress . . . and she's turned away from us, we can't see her, just a bit of one side of her face, and her head is slightly bowed. I wonder what that was about" (69). Not surprisingly, Mary is drawn to the lone figure mostly hidden from view, for she has always perceived herself in these terms—an independent women not defined by the roles typically assigned to women as mothers, domestic laborers, and grandmothers. Mary's own story has been one of gaps and mysteries. Even the odd number of scenes in the play, eleven, suggests that the block quilt of Mary's life is still being made. The act of rediscovering the family quilt provides yet another opportunity to articulate her identity, telling the employee, "I'm Mary Page Marlowe," and embracing the notion that one's identity is never fully understood by others or even the self.

Throughout the play, Mary's "panels" serve as demonstrations of her agency, weaving her own story and articulating her struggles as a woman. Even though the idealizations of marriage and motherhood often become vehicles for patriarchal oppression, Letts does not present women as helpless victims. Like the tarot reading and her guilty plea, Mary takes responsibility for who she is and for her actions. Doing so leads her to accept herself—including all of her successes and failures. It leads her to find a third husband—a fulfilling, healthy relationship. And it carries her to a place where she can view her life as well-lived: "I've had a *good* life" (39). She considers her third marriage and motherhood a positive part of that journey: "I wasn't a *great* mom. But I liked it" (40). She goes on to emphasize the pride and pleasure she took in her work as a CPA: "Client comes in, drops a shoebox full of paperwork on the desk . . . but then you start to get into that shoebox . . . like working a puzzle and putting the pieces in place—and sometimes it all comes together. All the numbers add up . . . No. The numbers do not always add up" (40). Like quilting, Letts presents accounting as another image for something fragmented and in need of assembling. Mary's journey to understand the self has been one in which the numbers often did not add up, but this reference to her career highlights the importance for women to cultivate identities outside of the home. Her professional pride reveals a need to balance work with personal expression (often through art), and it suggests that identity is too multifaceted to be defined by one characteristic or quality. It is a journey that requires assembly, community, and voice.

CHAPTER 6

Troubled Masculinity and Aging White Men in *Linda Vista,* *Superior Donuts,* and *Man from Nebraska*

In the fourth season of the television series *Mad Men,* Donald Draper (Jon Hamm) decides to take control of his unravelling life. The financial instability of his new advertising firm, blackout drinking, and a recent divorce have pushed him to the breaking point. He cuts back on alcohol. He starts swimming on a daily basis. And he even keeps a journal for self-reflection. One of his first entries includes a list of things he aspires to do: "I want to gain a modicum of control over the way I feel. I want to wake up. I don't want to be that man" ("Summer Man"). In essence, Don is perpetually on the run—from his marriages, his responsibilities as a father, and his shame for assuming a dead man's identity to escape the Korean War. Don's desire to be a different man points to his own concerns about masculine identity and to the show's broader deconstruction of conventional masculinity. These hard-drinking, promiscuous "ad men" don't find happiness. They watch their marriages fall apart, health deteriorate, friendships fragment, and careers become increasingly unfulfilling. Ultimately, *Mad Men* exposes this brand of manhood as a fantasy with devastating consequences.

The aging protagonists of Tracy Letts's *Linda Vista* (2017), *Superior Donuts* (2008), and *Man from Nebraska* (2003) struggle with similar concerns, and like Don they desire to be different men. This begins a process of self-discovery that reveals contemporary masculinity to be incongruent with nineteenth- and early twentieth-century conceptualizations of white manhood. To be fair, Letts's male characters have come a long way. They share little in common with the cowboys and tough guys that populate the works of David Mamet and Sam Shepard. Letts's Dick Wheeler, Arthur Przybyszewski, and Ken Carpenter don't assert their heterosexuality by demeaning gay men, for example. They don't try to dominate the opposite sex or feel threatened by professional women. And they don't rely on violence to prove their own toughness. Even Arthur's lugubrious fight in *Superior Donuts* occurs on behalf of Franco, not himself, and Wheeler's threats to defend Minnie from her abusive boyfriend in *Linda Vista* are never put to the test. In fact, these characters don't view manhood in terms of the binaries that trouble so many men on the American stage: masculine versus feminine, heterosexual versus homosexual, tough versus weak. So if Letts's men, all of whom are in their fifties, are so comfortable in their masculinity, why are they so miserable?

The answer stems, in part, from anxieties about parenting and whiteness. Just as Wheeler's deteriorating hip leaves him hobbling by the end of *Linda Vista,* he is hobbled by ongoing resentments about his shifting role from husband to father. Arthur in *Superior Donuts* has a similar experience at home, and his willingness to act as surrogate father for Franco raises troubling questions about the wife and daughter he abandoned five years earlier. And Ken's journey from Nebraska to London reveals an emotional distance between himself and his family that needs repair. In each play, the damaged family emerges as an image for frayed emotional bonds that inhibit male characters from viewing fatherhood as a positive part of masculine identity. At the same time, some of this unhappiness comes from racial biases, and their relationships with people of color suggest that white men need to eschew racial entitlement to find contentment. Wheeler's Vietnamese neighbor Minnie, Arthur's African American employee Franco, and Tamyra's friendship with Ken challenge these men to recognize the realities of racism in the United States. Whether it involves harboring stereotypes about Asian women, withdrawing from social activism, or maintaining a self-serving blindness about inequality, Letts's protagonists gradually come to terms with white privilege and discover art as a tool for achieving meaningful connections with others. Wheeler returns to photography after Minnie leaves him. Arthur picks up a pen to help Franco recreate his novel, and Ken takes sculpting lessons. Not only do these creative acts provide an outlet for self-expression, but their link with ethnic bias also presents art as a necessary tool for forging a masculinity defined by social equality, community, and cultural understanding. Through the lens of masculinity studies, this chapter examines Letts's portrait of contemporary white masculinity and the possibility contained within art to provide men with greater insight into the self and into what it means to be parents and white men in a nation of immigrants.

Masculinity Studies and White Men

Written in August 2018 and released in January 2019, the American Psychological Association published "Guidelines for the Psychological Practice with Boys and Men," a pamphlet addressing some of the social and psychological challenges linked with conventional understandings of manhood. The report argues, in part, that "traditional masculinity ideology has been shown to limit males' psychological development, constrain their behavior, result in gender role strain and gender role conflict, and negatively influence mental health and physical health" (3). It notes that boys, for instance, are more often diagnosed with learning difficulties in school. Young men tend to avoid seeking mental health treatment, having learned "from an early age . . . to minimize and manage their problems on their own" (3). And adult males remain four times more likely to commit suicide than women. As this data suggests, masculine identity continues to be fraught with personal difficulties, unrealistic expectations, and severe social consequences.

The men's liberation movement of the 1970s sought to address these types of problems by seeking a new definition of manhood.[1] In part, it took to heart the challenges posed by feminist, gay rights, and civil rights activists to white male power structures. It used them as models for examining the cultural construction of masculinity, arguing for the inclusion of men in discussions of gender identity, and it found inspiration in feminism's use of personal narratives to undermine generalizations about women's lives. More specifically, this movement rejected male sex-role theory as popularized by contemporary sociological and psychological writings such as Deborah David and Robert Brannon's *The Forty-Nine Percent Majority: The Male Sex Role* (1976). This book contends that power, wealth, success, aggression, risk-taking, and emotional inexpressiveness characterize masculinity. Such unrealistic standards, the men's liberation movement argued, led to psychological despair and social marginalization. The most significant scholarly challenge to this theory came a few years later with Joseph Pleck's *The Myth of Masculinity* in 1981. His examination of the "Male Sex Role Identity" pinpoints the contradictory messages of this myth as the primary source of anxiety in men's lives: "sex role identity prevents individuals who violate the traditional role for their sex from challenging it; instead, they feel personally inadequate and insecure—the subjective experience of sex role strain" (160).

Along with the work of Marc Fasteau and Jack Sawyer in the 1970s, Pleck's research helped launch the field of masculinity studies in the 1980s. In 1985 Eve Sedgwick, for example, examined the way men in British literature mediate or triangulate same-sex desire through women, offering a powerful model for integrating feminism and queer theory into the study of masculinity.[2] Two years later, Harry Brod's *The Making of Masculinities: The New Men's Studies* explored the "varying social-historical-cultural formations" shaping the male experience (40). According to Brod, the prominent role of men throughout history ironically rendered their private lives invisible, and this incongruity necessitated bringing the lived experiences of most men into broader discussions of gender. Raewyn (R. W.) Connell's concept of "hegemonic masculinity," which was introduced in the 1980s to challenge sex-role theory, complicated the category of "traditional" masculinity as well. For Connell, a complex interplay exists among gender, race, and class. As she explains in *Masculinities,* "hegemonic masculinity can be defined as the configuration of gender practice . . . which guarantees (or is taken to guarantee) the dominant position of men and the subordination of women" (77). Not only is this expression of manhood shaped by historical and cultural context, but it is also performative. Whether through bodybuilders in the mold of Arnold Schwarzenegger or the fictional heroes celebrated in Westerns and action films, most men try to emulate the types of manhood exalted in popular culture.[3]

An increased interest in the various forces shaping masculinity continued into the 1990s and early twenty-first century through the work of scholars such as Sedgwick, Brod, Connell, Michael Kimmel, and others. Kimmel's *Manhood in America: A Cultural History* (1996), for instance, traces the history of the "self-made man" as enshrined by the fiction of Horatio Alger. He argues that fears of failure and weakness have always haunted the promise of upward mobility in America, shaping men's actions in harmful ways. Men often feel the need "to *control themselves* . . . [to] project their fears onto *others;* and . . . [to] attempt an *escape*" (9). Kimmel concludes that men must forge a democratic masculinity instead. This vision of inclusivity offers the possibility of linking "what it has historically meant to be a man—strength, a sense of purpose, a commitment to act ethically, controlled aggressiveness, self-reliance, dependability— . . . with such newer masculine virtues as compassion, nurturing, and a fierce egalitarianism" (334). His recent book *Angry White Men: American Masculinity at the End of an Era* (2013) examines the dangers of rejecting such egalitarianism through his portrait of white male anger from school shootings and spousal abuse to white supremacy. These enraged responses to the socioeconomic opportunities available to women and people of color stem, in part, from "aggrieved entitlement," the belief that white men should continue to be the beneficiaries of power, wealth, and elevated social status. This ideology of privilege prevents white men from "[embracing] a new definition of masculinity, decoupled from that false sense of entitlement" (284). Increased equality, Kimmel concludes, not only alleviates anger but also benefits society as a whole.

Contemporary literature, by contrast, often portrays men in ways that diverge sharply from these psychological and sociological studies. As Alex Hobbs has argued, "literature champions a different model of masculinity"; it exposes the "gulf between the forms of masculinity that Connell and men's studies theorists more generally assert are culturally celebrated in America, especially in advertising and Hollywood movies, and the protagonists of American literature" ("Masculinity Studies," 387). One notable example of this tension can be found in the evolution of the Western. Cowboy masculinity typically asserts the dominance of white, Protestant men through the violent subordination of other groups such as women, ethnic minorities, and gay or effeminate men. According to Lydia Cooper, however, the Western by the late twentieth century often "constructs masculinity as a set of performances that de-normalize assumptions about gender and its relationship with power, specifically through unlinking idealized masculine performance from hegemonic power over others" (4). Maggie McKinley's examination of violence in American fiction from the 1950s to the 1970s finds a similar pattern. From Ralph Ellison to Philip Roth, characters that rely on violence to affirm their masculinity only "mire themselves more deeply within the racial and gendered conflicts that trigger their masculine anxiety" (4). As these trends suggest, contemporary American literature considers "macho" masculinity problematic. It exposes the performative nature of this construction as harmful and self-destructive, suggesting the need to radically revise this understanding of manhood.

Contemporary drama explores the legacy of hegemonic and cowboy masculinities as well. Much like the protagonists in Sam Shepherd's works, David Mamet populates his plays with high-strung men who ultimately reveal masculinity to be a site of contention and contradiction. As Arthur Holmberg has argued, Mamet's men "perform tough masculinity, but they strain, crack, and break. His plays capture the anger and fear and confusion about what it means to be a man today" (224). Letts's contribution to this critique comes not from cowboys and bruisers but from aging white men who have largely adapted to the changing gender and racial landscape of America.[4] Though his male characters remain aware of macho stereotypes, at times resorting to them out of desperation, they do not resist equality in their personal and professional lives. They have moved much closer to the democratic masculinity that Kimmel offers as the antidote to angry white men: "Equality, it turns out, is not a 'loss' for men, in some zero-sum calculus: it is a win-win. As women—and minorities and other 'others'—win, so too will angry white men. Ironically, increasingly equality will actually make us less angry" (Angry, 283). Letts's aging men reveal the challenges of achieving this egalitarian spirit, however. They harbor resentments about the transition from husband to father in marriage. They feel emotionally distant from their children. And despite their welcoming attitude toward other ethnic groups, they maintain a blindness to white patriarchal privilege that highlights the complexities of altering racist—and at times sexist—ideology. For Letts, these limitations not only create familial turmoil, but they also position the broken family as a representation of fractured communities in the United States. The solution that emerges in these plays is art. Art forges connections with others while operating as a vehicle for achieving a self-reflective, compassionate masculinity. It proves essential for personal and social healing.

"Seeing Beyond Yourself": Masculinity, Race, and Photography in *Linda Vista*

Linda Vista, which premiered at Steppenwolf Theatre Company in 2017 and underwent significant revisions before its Los Angeles and New York productions two years later,[5] uses Dick Wheeler's broken marriage, messy romantic life, and abandoned artistry to comment on the sources of white male malaise in America. Wheeler's journey—and that of aging white men more broadly—involves learning to hear and see beyond himself. As Letts has noted about the protagonist's opinionated nature, "with the fifty-year-old white male, there is the presumption that anybody . . . cares about your opinion. Your opinion actually has no more or less validity than anybody else's, and we don't actually need to hear your stance on everything."[6] Wheeler must learn in the course of the play that listening requires viewing others as equals. It requires recognizing sexist and racist ideology in order to find a meaningful place in American society.

As a fifty-year-old divorcé who has just moved out of his ex-wife's garage and into a cheap apartment in Linda Vista, California, Dick Wheeler struggles with the challenges of navigating single life and of coming to terms with gender and racial biases. Early in the play, Wheeler's college friends, Paul and Margaret, set him up on a blind date with Jules, but even her experience as a life coach is no match for Wheeler. Her efforts to encourage his photography only inspire anger: "You don't know what you're talking about . . . I'm no good." Ultimately, he destroys their romance with self-hatred, cynicism, and dishonesty about an affair with Minnie, a twenty-six-year old Vietnamese woman from his apartment complex. Minnie, who finds herself pregnant, abandoned by her abusive boyfriend, and broke, implores Wheeler to let her stay at his place at the end of the first act. What begins as a gesture of generosity turns into a sexual relationship that convinces Wheeler to help raise her unborn child. This impulse stems, in part, from his view of himself as a failed father. He plays no active role in the life of his thirteen-year-old son, Gabe. Instead, Wheeler hopes to start over as a parent. Eventually, he finds himself abandoned by Minnie, rejected by Jules (whom he begs for a second chance), and dismayed over the condition of his decaying hip. In the closing moments, Wheeler picks up a camera for the first time in nearly seventeen years and asks his coworker, Anita, for permission to take her picture. The shift from seeing Anita as a sexual object to treating her as an equal, from repairing broken cameras to engaging with the world as an artist, gives the audience some hope that Wheeler might find a more thoughtful, compassionate, and satisfying way to be a man.

Part of Wheeler's problem comes from sexually objectifying most of the women in his life, even though such impulses run counter to his political sensibility. On the surface, Wheeler's attitudes about women appear progressive. He firmly believes in abortion rights: "I think a woman should be able to terminate until the child can make a cogent argument in its own defense." He admires Margaret and Paul for not having children, and he supports the professional and intellectual aspirations of the women around him. Nevertheless, he has learned to link masculinity with sexual desirability, and he therefore evaluates women in the same terms. When moving into his new apartment, for example, Wheeler and Paul's banter captures the way sexual objectification shapes the male imagination. He describes a recent date with a Trump supporter as politically repugnant yet titillating: "This girl . . . my God. Like Ali MacGraw. I would have worn a MAGA hat if she had let me do all my dirty things." This reference to his boyhood fantasy about MacGraw sparks a debate over the actress's signature look, her hairstyle in different films, and her disclosure about being a sex addict. When the conversation turns to ridiculous celebrity endorsements from MacGraw to Joe DiMaggio, Wheeler begins singing the Simon and Garfunkel song "Mrs. Robinson" with the lyrics: "Tell us please, Joe DiMaggio, what it's like to fuck Marilyn Monroe. Oh, oh, oh." Ultimately, the humor in this scene underscores the difficulty of overcoming patriarchal modes of thinking. Both of these details—comparing his date to Ali MacGraw and thinking of Marilyn Monroe in terms of sex—highlight Wheeler's tendency to substitute sexual fantasies for reality. His impulse to subordinate a woman's individuality to her sexuality reflects culturally ingrained attitudes that encourage objectification, and Letts presents this as one of the problems that men need to overcome in the twenty-first century.

The treatment of Anita, the college dropout who works at the same camera repair store as Wheeler, offers another example of this dilemma. After accepting Paul's description of her as a brunette à la Ali MacGraw and discussing her "ample" breasts, Wheeler witnesses her daily harassment by Michael, the store's owner. He leers as she cleans the countertop and opens the door for customers, muttering to Wheeler: "My God, I jerked off last night just thinking about those tits . . . I think she wants me to take her back to my office and fuck her." Wheeler subtly mocks this interpretation but does nothing to discourage him. Instead, he tacitly accepts such commentary as part of workplace culture. At the end of the play, after learning about his son's obsession with the humiliation porn site Semen Disposal Units, however, Wheeler cannot tolerate Michael's recounting of a crime show in the style of *Law and Order: Special Victims Unit*. The plot, which involves a woman being held captive as a sex slave, becomes a way for Michael to discuss whether or not women enjoy being sexually dominated. Wheeler explodes at this moment, demanding an apology, quitting his job, and inadvertently forcing Anita to do the same. Wheeler's anger has numerous sources. Most notably, Michael's behavior gives Wheeler a disconcerting glimpse into what his son could become. Just as the objectification of women is condoned in popular culture from television to pornography, it is also passed on generationally, and Letts suggests that Wheeler—like all fathers—has a responsibility to teach his son better. Wheeler is also disgusted with himself here. He, too, has viewed Anita in demeaning ways, accepting Michael's antics until now. This breaking point underscores the play's message about the misogyny and sexism at the heart of patriarchal ideology. It is something that needs to be recognized and broken if men wish to achieve healthy relationships with women and to forge a positive model for manhood in the future.

Letts also uses Wheeler's bravado in this scene to undercut macho stereotypes as failed expressions of masculinity. After losing her job, Anita's frustration with Wheeler prevents any reading of his blowout with Michael as heroic or manly: "You think I can't manage Michael? I manage some version of Michael every day. I manage him when I'm in line for coffee, when I ride the bus, when I go to the beach. I managed a lifetime of Michaels before you ever came along." Wheeler's clichéd performance of defending a woman's honor and threatening violence on her behalf ("If you punish this girl, I'm going to come back here and kick your fucking ass.") ends up harming Anita. This brand of manhood ignores her agency and needs, and Wheeler lamely admits that he had not considered the repercussions of his actions. Furthermore, her comments about a lifetime of Michaels reinforces Letts's broader condemnation of sexism and misogyny. Anita's inability to buy a cup of coffee or take public transportation without being harassed draws attention to the need for cultural as well as ideological change. In effect, Wheeler's decision to "defend" Anita proves to be the opposite side of the same coin as Michael's harassment. Both subordinate a woman's interests to male needs for control and power. Yet by framing the play with Wheeler and Anita's relationship, Letts allows the audience to witness the protagonist's shift from sexually objectifying women to forging a friendship based on mutual respect. He not only gets Anita's permission to take her picture, but when she asks where to look, he responds, "Look wherever you want." This exchange, like the trajectory of their relationship, becomes a model for the journey white men need to take in America.

Racism in the play emerges as another impediment to male happiness. Once again, like his opinion on abortion, Wheeler possesses seemingly progressive attitudes about race. He rails against the intolerance of Trump voters, for instance: "The problem with these racist cocksuckers who voted for Trump isn't that they're doing too much OxyContin, it's that they need to do a whole lot more." He rejects the notion of finding a middle ground with them, yet Wheeler's enlightened perspective comes into question during his first encounter with Minnie. While waiting at a restaurant bar to interview for a job, Minnie finds herself the unwitting subject of Wheeler's attention. She soon recognizes him from his flirtatious behavior at the pool of their apartment complex and accuses him of hitting on her as well: "Don't sweat it, Dick. You're not my first Rice King today. You're not my first since I walked in this dump." She reduces Wheeler to a type on two levels here. First, she attributes his interest to a fetish, highlighting ethnic stereotypes as a daily burden for many Asian women. His initial confusion about the term "Rice King" also points to the failure of white men, such as Wheeler, to recognize the racist implications of eroticizing ethnicity. Minnie then mocks his poolside outfit, a speedo and Guayabera shirt, to level the playing field a bit, calling attention to the way his demeanor makes him a cliché of white, middle-aged masculinity. Wheeler does not respond by admitting bias on his part. Instead, angry with being reduced to a stereotype, he lashes out with a racist generalization: "You from here? . . . Are your parents boat people? Mom and Dad came over on the boat. Got married at nineteen. Your mom works at a nail salon, and Dad is a hard-ass small business owner of what—a Pho shop? . . . No, stop me when I'm wrong." This moment points to the way racism acts as a barrier between them. His narrative reduces all immigrants to the same set of experiences, and it makes her a vessel for his projections and assumptions about Asians.

Like his reliance on stereotypes, Wheeler's refusal to acknowledge ethnicity as a significant part of Minnie's identity offers another example of this problem. After their first sexual experience, Minnie questions Wheeler's declarations of affection: "Wake up, Dick. Life looks kind of sweet here with a pretty girl in your bed, in the moonlight, in Linda Vista. But you are a fifty-year-old man, and I'm not a doll. I'm not your sweet Asian flower." The term "Asian flower" again captures Wheeler's failure to see stereotypes as shaping his view of her. He does treat her as a doll, as something to protect, and he fails to connect his paternalism to race: "I'm not a fool. But Minnie provokes something . . . *protective* in me." Wheeler expresses this protectiveness largely by being a financial provider.

Unlike her tenuous status as an unemployed, first generation immigrant without a place to stay, however, Wheeler occupies a privileged position of authority as a white man with a job and a home. Minnie points out this power discrepancy before leaving him: "Even the first night it was like, what am I supposed to do? Reject you? And then where am I? I didn't have any place to go. No money. Nothing." At the same time, Minnie reminds Wheeler that his interest in her is rooted in fantasy. As Letts's characterization and the Steppenwolf production make clear, Minnie never plays into the stereotype of Asian women as demure. Minnie is brash, direct, loud, and not afraid to let everyone know when she needs to "take a shit."

Just as masculinity must break free from the stereotypical expectations of sexual prowess, violence, and money, it must also be devoid of racism, and Letts communicates this message most explicitly through Minnie's real name and her decision to speak Vietnamese at the end of the play. During an afternoon picnic, Margaret inquires about Minnie's background:

MARGARET: Your real name isn't Minnie, is it?
MINNIE: Chun Bien.
MARGARET: Chun is your family name.
MINNIE: Right.
WHEELER: I didn't know that.
MARGARET: You probably didn't ask.

Wheeler's ignorance here certainly supports Margaret's critique of his behavior: "It chaps my ass to see you with this girl instead with whom you have no connection, no affinity, no feeling, no empathy, nothing . . . She is everything you want in a playmate. Someone you can dress up with." His lack of interest in her name not only reflects his view of her as a type, but it also offers an implied critique of assimilation—or at least the expectation on the part of white America for nonwhites to erase aspects of their cultural identity for acceptance. In short, Minnie's Vietnamese heritage has been irrelevant to Wheeler. He even tries to render it invisible by suggesting humorous baby names like Horton Heat and Kid Lightning.

Not surprisingly, Minnie explains her decision to leave Wheeler in terms of ethnic identity. She argues that cooking at home with him, listening to his music (i.e., Steely Dan), and watching Wheeler's favorite Stanley Kubrick movies have come at the expense of her sense of self. She even notes Wheeler's disconnection from the baby: "You're in love with some idea about him, but one day he is going to be a real person . . . And maybe some of that is my fault. I mean what they went through. Things they sacrificed. I have to make good choices for this baby." The slip here from talking about Wheeler to referencing her parents is revealing. Minnie asserts the importance of her heritage—a heritage that her son will need to access one day—as part of the problem with their relationship. Wheeler continues to minimize this concern, however, offering her money and begging her to stay. After she steps outside of his apartment and he begins to hold her, she pleads with him to let go. She can only break away when she yells at him in Vietnamese, translating her words before walking off: "I am a person! And I say what I do." It is both a moment of agency and a statement about identity. It forces Wheeler to consider his blindness to the cultural barriers—just like the generational barriers—that prevent them from understanding each other.

While Letts presents transcending gender and racial bias as essential for achieving a more positive expression of masculinity, he also suggests that art needs to play a central role in this process. Wheeler's embittered relationship with photography comes from abandoning his career as a photographer for the *Sun Times* and from hosting a failed exhibition of his work: "I put some photos in a gallery, some bullshit theme, wine and cheese, whatever the fuck, and the needle didn't move. Pretty much nobody came. I didn't sell anything." Convinced of his own mediocrity, he claims that "Photography is light . . . And you're either Dorothea Lange or Gordon Parks or Diane Arbus, and you can capture that light to express a point of view. Or you're just one of the few billion assholes pushing a button on a phone a hundred times a day." Jules challenges this critique for leaving out the emotional dimension of art. She finds joy, for example, in the way karaoke celebrates song as a natural part of human expression and the way vulnerable acts, like singing, offer the power to "gain access to your internal self." This enables her to view "a photograph as a catalyst for seeing beyond yourself." Her definition of photography is an explicit criticism of Wheeler's narcissism here, but it also captures Letts's message about art as an important vehicle for masculinity. By abandoning his passion for photography, Wheeler has lost the ability to see others and himself with clarity. He has lost any understanding of art as having personal value even if it is not met with public acclaim or financial success.

Despite Wheeler's assessment of his work as "shallow and insipid," his discussion of one photograph captures the kind of connectivity with others and with one's own children that Letts presents as essential for contemporary masculinity. During their first night together, Jules asks Wheeler about a photograph of a little girl. He recalls the encounter in a Greek hospital when his wife got dysentery on their honeymoon. While looking for a cup of coffee, he ended up in the children's ward by accident:

> WHEELER: I was standing at the end of this long aisle between rows of hospital beds with sick children. At the other end of the aisle, I saw this little

girl, a patient. She saw me and broke into a huge smile and went into a dead run. Right for me. I bent down, and she threw her arms open, and I opened my arms and scooped her up and held her.

JULES: What was going on there?

WHEELER: I don't know. We didn't talk. The nurse came and took her from me. And I took that picture. [*Tearing up.*] I'm sorry [...] I've been sad for a while.

Photography operates on several important levels here. It can be a source of joy. The girl's reaction stems, in part, from being the subject of his attention, and Wheeler is moved by the memory of her unqualified affection. It also becomes an outlet for healing. Just as she experiences happiness despite her illness, art still has the potential to heal Wheeler. Much of his sadness comes from the frustrations of parenthood: "*And then Gabe was born!* And I got resentful. Not only of her attention to him but the structure of our lives." These feelings were exacerbated by the move from Chicago to California, which precipitated Wheeler's abandonment of photography. Finally, this picture, taken while the girl was being carried away, captures a moment of loss. It functions as a metaphor for the ways Wheeler has been frozen by loss since the birth of his son. His ability to pick up a camera at the end of the play, however, suggests a thawing out. It offers the possibility that he might be able to engage with the world and with his son meaningfully.

Part of this engagement involves his perception of ethnicity, and this photograph bridges cultural, ethnic, and linguistic barriers as well. Wheeler cannot communicate with the girl or the nurse, yet art has connected him to her indelibly. This momentary bond transcends his foreignness as a tourist, and the image becomes a reminder of the power of human connections—between cultures, between men and women, and between parents and children. Like Wheeler's ability to consider Anita's willingness to have her picture taken at the end of the play, photography might help him see people from other cultures and ethnicities not through the lens of prejudice or white privilege but on their own terms. Letts presents this as crucial for achieving a masculinity defined by community, empathy, and understanding.

Draft Dodgers, Dads, and Donuts: Manhood and Race in *Superior Donuts*

Letts's 2008 play *Superior Donuts* offers a meditation on aging masculinity, racism, and fatherhood through fifty-nine-year-old Arthur Przybyszewski, a Polish American donut shop owner in Chicago who came of age during the civil rights movement and the Vietnam War. As Letts explains, men like Arthur "were romantics, and like most romantics, reality did some damage to them. I was curious about that generation of men, and how they were dealing with that damage now, forty years later, as that particular class of boomers leaves middle age and enters into their old age."[7] The legacies of Vietnam and African American civil rights loom large in Arthur's understanding of white masculinity. His inertia in life, as captured by the decaying donut shop, is rooted in fear—of change, of loss, and of what dodging the draft in 1968 continues to say about him as a man. The U.S. wars in Afghanistan and Iraq serve as nagging reminders of his own choices regarding Vietnam, and the ethnic diversity of Uptown Chicago makes racial tension part of everyday life at the shop. Much like Wheeler's divorce in *Linda Vista,* broken families in *Superior Donuts* represent the way patriarchal modes of thinking and racist ideology fragment society. Arthur, who has watched his wife and daughter disappear from his life, remains haunted by his father's disapproval and his own abandonment of civil rights activism. Letts uses these tensions to present traditional standards of masculinity and racial inequity as impediments to the happiness of white men. Ultimately, he makes art—in this case, writing—the vehicle for forging a masculine identity that facilitates self-acceptance, self-sacrifice, and community.

At the opening of the play, Arthur's donut shop has been vandalized by someone who has spray painted the word "PUSSY" on the wall. His seeming indifference to the crime reflects a broader passivity on his part. Like his faded Grateful Dead T-shirt and hippie attire, Arthur appears stuck in time. He watches Superior Donuts, the store his father started sixty years earlier, slowly decline like himself, and his apathy stands in stark contrast to almost everyone around him. His Russian neighbor, Max, for example, owns an electronics business that he desperately wants to expand: "I come to this country to make a mark, not fade away" (30). Franco, the twenty-one-year old black man whom he hires to work in the shop, has visions of transforming Superior Donuts into a college-style coffee lounge with poetry readings, music, and some healthy eating options. And even Randy, a neighborhood police officer, shows a persistent romantic interest in Arthur despite her fear of rejection. Arthur's central dilemma comes from viewing himself as a failed man. In his youth, he evaded the draft in protest of the war, but he cannot reconcile these strong political convictions with his feelings of fear at the time—of fighting in the war, of being caught for fleeing the country, and of his father's view of him as a coward. When Franco's gambling debt results in a bookie cutting off three of his fingers and destroying the only copy of his novel, *America Will Be,* Arthur decides to act. He pays the debt, and in a messy, drawn-out act of fisticuffs, Arthur beats up the bookie. The play ends with him finding the courage to ask Randy on a date and assuming the role of surrogate father to help Franco rewrite his "great American novel."

As the profanity scrawled inside Superior Donuts suggests, Letts uses Arthur's history of draft dodging as a way to challenge the link between toughness and manhood in American culture. Arthur got caught up in the fervor for social change in the 1960s, joining marches and protests that once landed him in jail. After posting bail, however, his father's silence signaled a profound disappointment in the man Arthur was becoming. He drove his son to an Army recruitment office the same day, sending a clear message about masculine duty. Arthur's father, a prisoner of war during World War II and an immigrant who came to America with neither money nor the ability to speak English, modeled manhood through action, not words. He could not understand protesting against the United States instead of fighting for it, nor could he accept Arthur's decision to flee to Canada after receiving a draft notice. His last word to his son, "coward," continues to shape Arthur's view of himself as a failed man. In part, Arthur cannot reconcile his antiwar politics with the feelings of shame and fear they evoke: "What I did is called 'evasion.' Not resistance. Draft evaders are different from draft resisters. And what's the difference? The fight is the difference. Resisters fight. Evaders evade" (35). This act of evasion becomes the touchstone for Arthur's subsequent approach to life. He evades the responsibilities of family, letting his wife and daughter move to North Carolina without protest. He evades the modern world by maintaining a dingy donut shop while the Starbucks across the street takes more and more of his customers. And he evades friendships and romantic entanglements by refusing to open himself up to anyone. It is no accident that a former employee, who supports the current U.S. wars in the Middle East, writes "pussy" in the shop. The emasculating term captures the cultural traditions that associate masculinity with action, aggression, and violence. To run from a fight is to abandon one's manhood, and Arthur has accepted this perspective of himself.

Letts also uses Arthur's shame over his fear to critique constructions of masculinity that deny men a full range of emotional expression. Arthur recalls writing protest articles in Canada and spending time with other members of the Union of American Exiles. Though he characterizes the group as angry and righteous, he admits to feeling afraid: "We were all keeping a big secret, too: We were scared. I was ashamed of it then. Maybe I'm ashamed of it now. But really . . . What could be more human . . . To be scared . . . To keep it a secret" (35). The word "masculine" could be substituted for "human" here. Just as fear makes Arthur feel like less of a man than his father, this narrative of emotion provides a different path for understanding manhood. Culturally, men are not supposed to experience fear, and if they do, these feelings should remain a secret. Yet Letts insists on the term "human" to suggest that acts of emotional suppression compromise one's humanity. Arthur's silences about his family and feelings, for example, only prove isolating. Franco's references to Arthur's daughter shut off intimacy between them: "Right, if I mention her, I'm just an employee" (50). And in the face of Arthur's seeming emotional indifference, Randy snaps at her partner before storming out of the store: "He knows we care about him. We don't have to spell it out for him . . . So I think it's pretty clear he's not interested in us!" (48). As these exchanges imply, men need to express their emotions in order to connect with others.

Still under the shadow of his father's view of masculinity, Arthur insists on a physical fight with Lester to prove himself as a man, but Letts undermines this effort by using it as a metaphor for the value of taking emotional risks. In the production notes, the playwright provides numerous details about the altercation between two aging men, describing it as labored, clumsy, "painful," "sweaty," and "bloody." He also wants the fight to be uncomfortably long for the audience, outlining phases that include surprise, agility, fatigue, and bloodied exhaustion. Most important, Letts notes that Luther is clearly the better fighter in terms of experience and physical condition, but Arthur prevails "because of his strength of purpose . . . and Luther's ulcer" (59). Letts's choreography is antithetical to the fighting sequences in most Hollywood films, for its awkward ugliness prevents any interpretation of it as heroic. Even though Arthur wins, everyone questions the fight's purpose and value. Arthur is the first to admit that "I don't know if it did any good," and Max responds by reducing it to entertainment: "Maybe not for you. But I sure got the charge" (60). Repeated references to *Rocky* in this scene further mock the way Hollywood aggrandizes male violence. In the world of *Superior Donuts,* fighting accomplishes nothing tangible. Luther continues as a bookie who uses violence to collect money, even at the expense of his worsening ulcer, and the damage to Franco's hand cannot be undone. Nevertheless, the fight becomes a way for Arthur to overcome his emotional paralysis. He learns that friendship and community come from engagement. When Arthur expresses fear about acting on Franco's behalf, he decides not to run away "because of that kid" (55). Franco inspires him to face his fear in the name of someone else, in the name of someone he believes in. Though the fight with Luther reminds Arthur that manhood does not need to be asserted through violence (he humorously places Luther's money in a Kotex box), it does function as a metaphor for being willing to take the bruises that sometimes come from caring for others.

Through Arthur's connection with African American civil rights, Letts makes social activism central to the play's exploration of masculinity as well. In many ways, Arthur is much closer than Wheeler to embodying the type of white manhood that Letts celebrates. His attitude toward race differs from those around him who tend to reduce ethnic groups to stereotypes. Max, for example, assumes the donut shop was vandalized by "black son-of-bitches," and when Luther's henchman learns that Franco's father abandoned him, he mutters, "there's a shocker" (12, 38). Arthur, however, recognizes racial prejudice as a social problem that needs to be fixed. In his reflections on childhood, his memories capture the extent of the city's segregation: "Every Sunday hanging out in someone else's basement, food all day . . . Polish the only language I'd hear" (22). The civil rights movement "changed" this landscape, in part, by exposing the extent of racist practices in American life. Just as Arthur defined himself in contrast to his father's beliefs about Vietnam, race becomes another divisive issue for them after Martin Luther King's march in Marquette Park in 1966: "My mom got the old man drunk in the middle of the day to keep him from going down there and shaming us. Maybe that's where the trouble started with the old man" (22). Racism operates as a social as well as familial shame here, and it inspires Arthur to participate in the 1968 marches on the Civic Center after King's assassination. For Letts, Arthur's willingness to protest injustice emerges as the real model for masculinity. Taking shared responsibility for social wrongs makes Arthur's display of manhood more ennobling than that of his father—who merely wishes to quell activism and to view war as patriotic.

His father's disapproval of these acts does have the power to derail Arthur, and Letts pinpoints Arthur's subsequent withdrawal from activism as the real source of his failed masculinity. The play first makes this message clear through Franco's explicit, often humorous observations about racial prejudice in America. Franco offers ongoing commentary about racial injustice. While applying for the job at Superior Donuts, he criticizes donuts and other processed foods for targeting black people and the poor: "It's not exactly a healthy choice . . . Which contributes to obesity and cardiac disease in the African American community" (19). He goes on to argue that poor black consumers cannot be blamed because society typically denies them healthier options: "You don't see no Whole Foods in this neighborhood, do you? . . . And you ain't never seen a brother in the Whole Foods, unless he's stockin' the shelves. Can you picture that, some big angry black man shoppin' in Whole Foods, his arms all loaded with soy cheese and echinacea and starfruit" (19–20). The humor in the juxtaposition of angry black men and these foods only adds validity to Franco's critique. They presumably don't eat soy cheese because corporations like Whole Foods do not tend to open stores in African American neighborhoods.

Like Franco, Arthur agrees that racist ideologies shape the white imagination, and he admits to possibly harboring them himself. When asked directly if he is racist, Arthur stammers, "No. I mean, I don't think so. I mean, I hope not. I mean, probably not, but . . . you know" (25). This response suggests an important self-awareness on his part. Arthur willingly engages in frank discussions about race and admits his own shortcomings. At the same time, after passing Franco's "racist test" by naming ten African American poets, Arthur attributes the knowledge to being "a reader, that's all" (31). This qualification ("that's all") underscores Letts's broader message about white masculinity. Recognizing personal bias is an important step in building a more accepting, equitable community for everyone, but as Arthur's history with the civil rights movement and reading habits suggest, he already possesses this knowledge. His failure is inaction. Listing these poets and recognizing the corporate exploitation of people of color do not bring about social change. Passivity and disengagement tacitly perpetuate prejudice, and the challenge for Arthur—like the generation of white men he represents—is acting on the principles of social justice.

Through Arthur's journey from bystander to caretaker, Letts presents art as the vehicle for achieving a masculinity defined by social engagement. Franco announces proudly on his first day of work that he has just completed the great American novel—*America Will Be*. This title, an allusion to the 1936 Langston Hughes poem "Let America Be America Again," comes from a narrator who laments the nation's failed promise of freedom. "I am the poor white, fooled and pushed apart, / I am the Negro bearing slavery's scars. / I am the red man driven from the land, / I am the immigrant clutching the hope I seek— / And finding only the same old stupid plan / Of dog eat dog, of mighty crush the weak." Hughes uses the disenfranchisement of various ethnic groups as a call to action—to forge a common purpose for achieving the ideals of the American project. Certainly, twenty-first century Chicago, as captured in *Superior Donuts,* is fraught with the types of racial and economic divisions referenced in the poem. The legacy of racism shapes how the characters see themselves and others, and Letts alludes to the hardships facing the African American community by characterizing the neighborhood as marked by vandalism, drug deals, and poverty. Franco's novel, however, becomes a vehicle for solidarity. After Arthur reads the book, Franco expresses his gratitude in terms that resonate with Hughes's poem: "Thanks, Arthur . . . That's what friends do, right? They share their stories" (43). Sharing stories builds friendships. It facilitates understanding across social and cultural lines. And it inspires meaningful engagement with social problems. As Arthur explains before his fight with Luther, "you humiliated that boy's body and you think you can justify that. But you can't justify destroying that kid's story" (57). Arthur recognizes that the destruction of the manuscript has implications outside of Franco. His story, like the broader role of art whether in the form of a poem or a play, can contribute to healing social divisions. Art's ability to resonate with audiences of different economic and ethnic backgrounds, in other words, makes it an invaluable tool for achieving an America that lives up to the ideals of egalitarianism.

By the end of the play, art has also inspired an expression of masculinity that embraces fatherhood and compassion. After Franco's release from the hospital, Arthur assumes the role of surrogate father, in part, to heal from some of the pain of being estranged from his daughter. As Arthur recalls, his wife, "Magda . . . begged me to talk, begged me to fight, but I couldn't do it" (43). To some extent, this stoicism comes from his sense of compromised masculinity. He has never been a fighter, so he resorts to another masculine cliché, silence, in the face of his disintegrating marriage. Like Wheeler, the problem for Arthur appears rooted in the way fatherhood changed marital life: "A child is born, and a kiss becomes a handshake, and you no longer cast a shadow in your own house. I didn't know you had to have hope to raise a kid. I didn't know you couldn't raise a kid without it" (51). When he no longer feels sexually desired by his wife, Arthur loses his last anchor to conventional masculinity. He likens himself to a ghost, for without words, action, or sexuality, he believes that he has no substance as a man. While this broken marriage serves as an image for Arthur's shattered sense of masculinity, Franco's book offers an opportunity for Arthur to align fatherhood with manhood. Its title, *America Will Be*, holds the promise not only of racial integration and equality but also of crafting a new vision for being a man. Just as Arthur finds a surrogate for his daughter in Franco, the play suggests the need for aging white men to offer a more inclusive vision of masculinity for future generations. Arthur's willingness to sacrifice for Franco and to become a father figure ("I'll take care of him") models a masculinity grounded in compassion and care.

Finally, Letts presents the shared act of artistic creation as a way to cultivate an image of compassionate masculinity. Throughout the play, the most significant disclosures about Arthur's life have come in the form of monologues addressing the audience, not other characters. This approach captures the extent of Arthur's unwillingness to open himself to others, and it reinforces his sense of hopeless isolation. Franco's novel, however, has taught Arthur the need to engage with others through shared stories. In the closing moments, he offers to do the same: "You don't know what I'm talking about, do you? Magda, or the war . . . my history. My parents. Maybe I can tell you about myself" (65). However, Franco's trauma—the loss of his fingers, the destruction of his manuscript, and the need for Arthur's financial assistance—prevents him from listening at this moment. His pain gives Arthur an important opportunity to help Franco restore his sense of masculinity through art. Taking out a pad and pen and sitting across the table from Franco, Arthur writes: "America . . . Will . . . Be." He not only acts as a caretaker in this moment, but he also eradicates hierarchies by assuming the role of taking dictation, of listening to and helping recreate Franco's story. Ultimately, this relationship makes Arthur recognize that his failure as a man came both from abandoning his efforts to fight injustice and from remaining emotionally disengaged from others. Letts leaves the audience with these two men—separated by generations, ethnicity, and class—coming together for each other: "We . . . both of us, we got helped." Stories and shared experiences build community. They foster greater transracial understanding. And they even forge a more positive expression of manhood in the process.

Sculpting Masculinity: Ethnicity and Art in *Man from Nebraska*

While travelling through Lincoln, Nebraska, Letts once observed an older married couple in a cafeteria, "not speaking to each other at all for the entirety of their meal. They were comfortable. It was a comfortable silence." The encounter inspired the thirty-six-year-old playwright to think about whether or not "everyone at some point in their lives . . . [asks] the big questions. Do we all have that moment where we look up and say, 'Why am I here? What am I doing here?' So I thought what if you put those questions in the mind of a person who seems least likely to have those questions."[8] This couple became the inspiration for *Man from Nebraska,* which premiered at Steppenwolf in 2003 and became a finalist for the Pulitzer Prize the following year. For Letts, Ken and Nancy Carpenter represent the Midwest, and one of the characters in the play even notes that Nebraska is "right in the middle" of the country (38). Their quintessential Americanness invites audiences to read Ken as an embodiment of aging white masculinity in America. Like Arthur, Ken possesses many male characteristics celebrated in Letts's later plays. He is capable of kindness and generosity. He opens himself to new experiences. And he tries to recognize his own cultural and racial biases. Ultimately, his crisis of religious faith enables Letts to critique standard expressions of masculinity, such as toughness and wanderlust, to expose the dangers of white privilege, and to present art as a crucial tool for understanding the self.

The quiet, steady life of Ken Carpenter, a fifty-seven-year-old family man, insurance agent, and member of his local Baptist church, is shattered upon the sudden realization that he no longer believes in God. With his mother dying in a nursing facility and his faith shaken by panic attacks, Ken admits to his wife that "we die . . . and we're done, no more [. . .]. Nobody listens when I pray. We're not rewarded for what we do right" (13). Ken attributes part of the problem to the tendency for self-examination to be submerged by the mundane: "My life, *way* of life, um . . . routines. My routine with your mother. [. . .] And the job, and the, the . . . town" (21). He is also troubled by the indoctrination of people—including himself and his children—into belief systems such as religion: "I think maybe I've just never considered it. I've always just accepted." When his minister recommends that Ken take a vacation, he chooses London, which "seemed like the right distance. Foreign but . . . not too foreign" (43). Ken soon finds himself on an adventure of self-discovery. He navigates a clumsy romantic encounter with a domineering businesswoman. He befriends a black cocktail waitress, Tamyra, in whom he confides daily, and he begins taking sculpting lessons from her flatmate, Harry. These experiences—like his reflections on serving in the Air Force—confront Ken with his blindness to white privilege. After returning to Nebraska for his mother's funeral, Ken feels empowered to assert more control over life. Art has inspired him to be closer with his daughters, to begin something new with his wife, and to reshape his identity as a white man.

Through Ken's crisis of faith, Letts offers a model for modern manhood based on the rejection of masculine clichés. When Reverend Todd advises Ken to take a vacation, for example, he encourages him to think of it in terms of cowboy masculinity:

> REVEREND TODD: Get the heck out of Lincoln . . . What books do you like? You a mystery reader? History buff?
> KEN: I like Westerns.
> REVEREND TODD: Now you're talking, old son. Grab a toothbrush, pack some clean shirts, some Louis L'Amour paperbacks, and get yourself gone. (32)

His reference to L'Amour, arguably the most prolific and influential writer of Westerns in the twentieth century, recommends a particular type of manly narrative for Ken. The Reverend even shares his own story of the rugged outdoors, recalling a sweaty, ten-hour battle to uproot an old tree stump. The Reverend claims kinship with L'Amour's cowboys here—men who know how to navigate the land, find water in a parched desert, ride horses with skill, and fight with a clear sense of right and wrong. Ken, however, is the antithesis of such a cowboy. He travels east instead of west. He has probably never raised his fists or voice in anger. And at this moment, his sense of right and wrong is utterly clouded by doubt. In these ways, Letts presents Ken's masculinity as more complex than L'Amour's heroes. It requires wrestling with internal rather than external challenges to find contentment.

Ken's more introspective approach to masculinity also gets contrasted with stereotypes about toughness, particularly as embodied by the military. Ken served in the Air Force, "between wars" (26), yet he finds its male ethos and community unappealing: "I don't like all those *men*. Everywhere you went there were all these *men* there. Men seem so dull after a while. And they're all the same, especially in the military, 'cause I guess they're supposed to be" (45).

Although part of Ken's distaste comes from all of the "cursing," "rotten food," and "the hours," he singles out uniformity as the biggest problem. Forged by drill sergeants and regimented schedules, most soldiers, according to Ken, fit the same mold of masculinity, and he has no desire to be this way. Instead, he befriends a fellow soldier from the South who enjoys silence: "We didn't mind being quiet together" (46). Ken ultimately considers the fraternal community of the military distasteful: "I just couldn't find a reason to spend time with those fellows. We had nothing to learn from each other" (46). For Ken, one learns from difference. He recognizes masculinity as multifarious and diverse, which military culture denies, and Letts uses this perspective to offer a view of manhood outside the clichés of cowboys and soldiers.

Letts provides another example of this contrast through Bud Todd, a seventy-five-year-old veteran of World War II. His perspective on mortality— "I've buried so many of my friends, I got calluses on my hands from carrying caskets" (79)—contributes to his talkative, funny, frank disposition. He is open about sexual desire, saying to Nancy with a wink that "These young folks get downright jumpy when the talk turns to S-E-X" (69). He pressures her to kiss him. And he argues that Ken will not come back because "it's a man's nature to strike out into the world, endeavor, explore" (81). Though these different approaches to masculinity are partially generational and circumstantial (Bud's crisis of faith came after resorting to cannibalism as a POW), Ken returns home. He does not try to insert himself into someone else's marriage, nor does he fall into generalizations about male wanderlust and adventure. His trip to London, which his minster advised, gives him a clearer sense of himself as a man. It helps him affirm commitment to family as a laudable masculine trait.

Even though Ken's crisis of faith makes him feel "ashamed" (25), his willingness to expose his vulnerabilities—to reject traditional modes of masculine expression—facilitates meaningful connections with others. The first instance occurs with Pat Monday, the executive who flirts with Ken on his flight to London and invites him over for a night of sex. In her apartment, she wrestles him to the bed, sticks her tongue in his mouth, and places his hands on her breasts. Meanwhile, she demands that he treat her like a sexual object: "I want you to do me like your whore . . . Show me I've been so bad" (51, 52). Her leather straps and restraints only make Ken more flustered as he tries to explain that his "heart's not in this" (52). Finally, he blurts out "no," describing himself as inexperienced and confused. He even admits that the idea of having sex with her frightens him. On the surface, this sexual role-play draws on elements of patriarchal culture that objectify women, yet Pat coopts this dynamic for her own pleasure. She assumes a domineering posture with Ken, providing the restraints and telling him what to do ("Show me." "Stick me." "Pinch my nipples."). In exasperation with his naïveté, she even explains, "You don't have to be [experienced] . . . I'm the woman. Goddamn it. I'll take care of everything" (52). For Pat, women bear the burden of caring for male needs, and the same proves true during her encounter with Ken. His refusal to participate in this performance necessitates her shift from one role (a type of dominatrix) to another (nurturer). This leads to a brief moment of tenderness between them, however: *"She holds him in an embrace. They slowly rock. They caress each other . . . backs, arms, necks. They kiss. [. . .] They kiss"* (53). Their implied sexual encounter may be a result of her taking "care of everything," but he at least offers a narrative for sex rooted in love and intimacy, not power.

In a similar way, Tamyra's friendship with Ken enables her to admire his openness to new experiences. She even calls him "very brave" at one point (76), using language more commonly associated with the heroics of cowboys and soldiers. Tamyra may not be interested in Ken romantically, but she does acknowledge that internal, emotional, and spiritual journeys require bravery. For Letts, Ken offers a portrait of manhood in which openness and bravery of spirit are rewarded with friendship. As he explains to his daughter, "I've made a couple of good friends here, whom I care about, and they inspire me" (72). This moment enables Letts to suggest that compassionate engagement with others can be a source of inspiration and community for men. It is a type of masculinity worth emulating.

Letts also uses Ken's relationship with Tamyra to pivot into the play's examination of white privilege. Despite Ken's positive attributes, he remains unaware of the way racism has limited his ability to form meaningful connections with nonwhites. Part of Ken's biases come from his lack of exposure to people of color in the Midwest. When he tells Tamyra about his friendship with an African American soldier in the Air Force, for instance, he considers this relationship the best part of his military experience: "One boy, a colored boy—a black boy, a young black man, from Oklahoma, named Eamonn Pitts . . . we got on pretty good 'cause we were from the same part of the country [. . .] I guess that's one of the good things about the military, 'cause a guy like me, where I come from and what I do, would never really have an opportunity to, to . . . uh, spend time with black people, hardly even see a black person, if it weren't for the Air Force. I had never really known black folks" (46). This initial description captures some of the challenges of overcoming racist ideology. While some of Ken's stammering comes from his discomfort in discussing blackness with Tamyra, his language, particularly the slip from "colored boy" to "black boy" to "black man," reflects hierarchies that have shaped his perception of African Americans. The term "boy" not only implies the subservient status of someone to care for or to command, but it also harkens back to Antebellum terminology designed to emasculate African American men. Even Ken's later admission that he and Eamonn "never spoke again after the service" (46) suggests race as a barrier between them. Ken does not view him as fully equal, which provides no basis for mutual acceptance and understanding. Finally, Ken's claim that Eamonn taught him grace seems problematic as well. Both Eamonn's upbringing in Oklahoma and his penchant for silence appealed to Ken, but the latter raises questions about his embodiment of grace. While "grace" refers to a refined or elegant bearing, it also describes a goodwill rooted in courteousness and respect. Applying this term to someone predominantly described as "quiet" and to whom Ken initially labels as "boy" does not endow Eamonn with much agency. It implies that Ken only takes comfort in African Americans who display a polite deference toward whites.[9]

Like Franco in *Superior Donuts,* Tamyra draws attention to the way racial hierarchies shape the black experience in Western culture. After Ken confesses his secret fantasies about freedom, she calls attention to the extent of his white privilege: "Free. You lack freedom, so you fantasize about it" (55). She uses this detail to contrast their lives, emphasizing the advantages that come from both his wealth and his whiteness: "I'm nice to you . . . because you tip well . . . Americans tip because Americans speak the language of money. That's your language, Ken. Money. You pay me to be nice to you" (56). Money, in other words, insulates Ken from the types of challenges facing Tamyra, and it enables him to establish the terms of his relationships with people of color by paying them for labor and even kindness. While Ken responds with surprise that she might not like him personally, she explains that his privilege prevents him from seeing her as a person: "I have a life of my own [. . .] With my very own problems and . . . inabilities. [. . .] The inability to make money. The inability to get out of this asinine job. [. . .] Pining for freedom when you have more of it than anyone in the history of this earth. [. . .] You sit there on your lily-white American ass and talk to me about freedom?" (56). By pointing out the tradition of power that benefits Ken and continues to subjugate people of color around the world, she contrasts his personal feelings of entrapment with the socioeconomic realities of oppression. As she explains, "Freedom only comes in one cast . . . You'd have to be denied it to know" (57). Ken's status as a white man means that he has never known oppression, and for Letts, recognizing such privilege is the starting point for building a multiracial community based on equality and empathy.

As with *Linda Vista* and *Superior Donuts,* art emerges in *Man from Nebraska* as the primary means for transcending white privilege and for building the types of cultural exchanges that lead to community and self-understanding. Letts initially casts Ken's journey in terms of art through his preference for fiction over poetry. As Tamyra observes, Ken takes comfort in stories: "Otherwise, how would you ever get from here to there" (40–41). His need for narrative mirrors his desire for clarity about what it means to be an aging white man in America. Sculpture offers him one pathway for doing so. According to the stage directions, Harry's stone sculpture features *a nude woman, her hands raised skyward in a gesture of supplication. Only the top half is completed; the lower half is merely an immense block of stone. It is apparent Tamyra is the model for this sculpture* (66). Tamyra's supplicant posture indicates a longing for answers, for help, and Ken bursts into tears upon seeing it. Though this artwork elicits a powerful emotional reaction from Ken, he merely sees himself at this moment. This sculpture does not give him insight into the experiences of others, for he still does not understand how Tamyra's desire for answers differs from his. Letts uses this failing as an image for the problem with white privilege—insularity.

Only when Ken begins sculpting does he recognize art's potential to forge connections across racial and cultural lines. Ken's struggles to replicate Tamyra stem, in part, from his lack of technical skill. He simply does not have the ability to shape and mold clay with precision. At the same time, his failure reflects an inability to understand the experiences of black women in Western culture. As his instructor Harry explains, art is an act of interpretation: "There is no point in producing Tamyra *again:* she already exists. I mean, yes, you want to have the *ability* to do that: that's *craft*. But your belief, your expression of your belief: that's *art*" (75). Interpretation, however, requires a deep understanding of the subject, and Ken primarily considers art a vehicle for seeing himself. So it comes as little surprise that his initial sculpture of her looks like a "self-portrait" (77). He may be able to produce only a vision of himself at this point, but in Letts's hands, the beauty here comes from Ken's willingness to try. His efforts at sculpting have built meaningful friendships with Tamyra and Harry. Art has not only made Ken part of a broader community, but it has also given him a new clarity about himself ("I feel less confused"). In these ways, it offers an important step in overcoming the types of biases that hinder community.

Throughout the play, the barriers associated with race and gender unfold alongside strains within the Carpenter family, and by linking the two, Letts makes Ken's return home an image for his willingness to overcome familial as well as cultural impasses. Early in the play, Ken expresses doubts about his parenting: "I'm thinking I didn't do a very good job with them . . . I wish I had done things different . . . I think my parents did a better job of raising me than I did of raising my own kids" (43). Some of this tension is evident in his daughters' responses to family matters. In reaction to Ken's trip, for example, Ashley advocates for divorce despite her mother's objection: "I'm sure it would

make you happy if I drew a line in the sand and vowed to divorce your father
if he crossed it . . . but I'm not built like that" (48). Natalie, by contrast, communicates her attitude through indifference: "She said [Ken's absence] wasn't
any of her business . . . She made some stupid speech about how we're all
'free agents'" (49). Natalie does not even bother to come home for her grandmother's funeral. In many ways, Ken's departure reveals the extent of the emotional distance between him and his children—or at least the fragility of these
bonds. Ashley goes so far as to tell him that he has "forfeited the right to ask"
about her kids and that she considers him a stranger (73). By offering to bridge
that distance through openness and intimacy ("That's my fault. We can change
that" [86]), however, Ken signals a sincere desire to connect with his daughter.
Early in the play, Ashley describes herself as his "friend," but to form that kind
of bond, Ken now realizes it requires a different kind of investment—the kind
he had to work for with Tamyra and Harry.

   Such moments resonate metaphorically as well. In the most explicit image
of fragmented familial bonds, his wife describes Ken's abandonment as having
torn up their marriage: "You tore it up . . . Now it's nothing . . . just pieces . . .
just scraps . . . ashes" (88). Ken, though apologetic, hopes these ashes are the
starting point for building something new. As he proclaims, "I don't know
where I want to go or what I want to do. But I want you with me. I want us to
be together" (87). This moment can be read as reflecting the need to tear up
white privilege in order to build a new social structure as well. Ken's willingness to transform his relationships with his family and to leave Nebraska ("I
don't know where I want to go") suggests a desire to maintain his friendships
with Tamyra and Harry. Unlike his memory of Eamonn Pitts, Ken seeks a new
community defined by emotional openness, multiculturalism, and art. It is an
affirming vision for Ken and the aging white man he represents.

White Masculinity in Twenty-First Century America

Near the end of *Linda Vista,* Paul offers Wheeler some advice: "You know
there's a price to pay for living your life the way you do. There is also a price
to pay for living life like me. Nobody gets out of this for free." In many ways
Linda Vista, Superior Donuts, and *Man from Nebraska* examine the challenges
and costs of being a man in twenty-first-century America. Even though Letts's
leading men do not succumb to the legacy of cowboy masculinity, they sometimes fall into male stereotypes in moments of crisis. These choices prove
disastrous, however. Wheeler's sexual affair with a twenty-six-year-old cannot
mitigate the realities of his aging body. Arthur's fight with Luther, like his stoicism, does not change anything. And Ken's abandonment of his wife, to deal
with problems on his own, only brings him full circle. For Letts, these failures

highlight the unrealistic and counterproductive ways popular culture has constructed white masculinity from action heroes and cowboys to hitmen and mobsters. They suggest that contemporary manhood is far too diverse and nuanced for such oversimplifications.

Instead, Letts aligns white aging masculinity with qualities such as openness, caring, generosity, and introspection. Once Wheeler stops viewing Anita as a sexual conquest, for example, he can build a friendship based on mutual respect. Arthur learns the value of sharing his life with others by becoming a father figure to Franco and by dating Randy. And Ken's generosity toward Tamyra and Harry, which stems from genuine friendship, inspires him to build a stronger bond with his wife and family. Throughout these relationships, Letts's male protagonists learn to recognize—and at times take responsibility for—their own faults. This willingness to question their motives and actions not only reflects a sincere attempt at self-improvement, but it also demonstrates a desire for change—change that has personal as well as social implications.

In their examination of masculinity, these plays also explore the way anxieties about aging and fatherhood operate as impediments to white male contentment. Wheeler's failure to take care of his hip, which leaves him hobbling in pain by the end of *Linda Vista,* offers the most notable example of this fear. Letts uses his damaged body as a call to see aging as a natural, positive part of masculine identity, not a source of shame or embarrassment. He communicates a similar message through his characters' relationships with women. All of the women in Wheeler's life, whether in his romantic history with Margaret, current affairs with Minnie and Jules, or Anita's fondness—consider him desirable. Randy in *Superior Donuts,* who follows up on the vandalism crime so frequently that "you'd think Lindbergh's baby got swiped out of your donut shop" (33), pines away for Arthur. And women are drawn to Ken as well, whether in his sexual encounter with Pat Monday or his friendship with Tamyra. Just as these men struggle to reconcile their masculinity with being in their fifties, they also tend to view their mistakes as parents as signs of personal failure. This attitude pushes them into abandoning their children. Wheeler, for instance, would rather raise a new baby with Minnie than confront Gabe's unhealthy interest in pornography, and both he and Arthur resent the way fatherhood replaced sexual intimacy with the day-to-day demands of childrearing. Even Ken, whose grown daughters and long-term marriage suggest stability, recognizes the emotional distance between him and his daughters. For Letts, these men need to learn to see parenting as an ongoing process that involves successes and failures. They need to accept fatherhood as an affirming part of their masculinity.

Their blindness to white privilege creates personal and social barriers for them as well. Wheeler declares his love for Minnie yet views her through stereotypes about Asian women. Arthur abandons his civil rights activism because of his shame over dodging the draft, and Ken has never maintained lasting friendships across racial lines. Only their interactions with people of different ethnicities force them to confront this privilege. Minnie has constructed her entire persona in response to stereotypes about Asian women, and she uses Vietnamese to break off her relationship with Wheeler. Franco's diatribes on racial bias in corporate America shine a light on the ubiquity of racism. Similarly, in a moment of shock over Ken's naïveté about race, Tamyra shares her views on freedom. These confrontations demand a recognition that building social equality starts with recognizing and dismantling one's own racist ideology.

Ultimately, real personal and social transformation seems possible only through art. It enables men to see beyond themselves—beyond pain, anxiety, fear, and loss—for long enough to recognize the needs of others. Wheeler must pick up his camera to break out of a state of narcissistic self-interest. Arthur's offer to help restore Franco's novel represents the importance of sharing stories. And Ken's sculptures make him realize that interpretation requires insight into the lives of others. Art also demands community. Just as Franco shares his novel with Arthur, Wheeler discusses his photography with Jules, and Ken needs to learn that art is about connection. As Tamyra explains, "None of it means anything without a witness" (77). Art, in other words, enables the kind of exchanges that build empathy and understanding. It bridges the gap between genders and races and ages. And for white men it becomes a way to help dismantle traditional masculinity and white privilege.

Women in Windows

In Alfred Hitchcock's 1954 masterpiece *Rear Window*, L. B. Jefferies' (James Stewart's) adventurous lifestyle as a globe-trotting photographer has left him with a broken leg. Stuck in a wheelchair for six weeks in a two-room apartment, he passes the time by watching his neighbors through a telephoto lens. One night he becomes convinced that neighbor Lars Thorwald (Raymond Burr) has murdered his wife. With the help of his girlfriend and his physical therapist, Jefferies begins gathering evidence to convince a New York City detective that a crime has actually taken place. Jefferies' theories get dismissed along the way as "wild opinions" and foolishness, in part because of his voyeurism. He violates the privacy of others every time he picks up his camera or a pair of binoculars. Hitchcock not only implicates the audience in these acts, as we watch along with the same guilty pleasure, but he also uses it to capture the film's message about surveillance and privacy. As Jeffries' physical therapist observes, "We've become a race of Peeping Toms. What people ought to do is get outside their own house and look in for a change." The detective echoes something similar after investigating Thorwald: "That's a secret, private world you're looking into out there. People do a lot of things in private they couldn't possibly explain in public." These moments certainly resonate with 1950s culture at the time. Alongside the investigations of the House Committee on Un-American Activities (HUAC), Joseph McCarthy's highly visible assault on Communism was designed to exacerbate Cold War fears. His inflammatory rhetoric gave the impression that threats to American democracy lurked everywhere—even the house next door. This climate of fear reached epic proportions by the middle of the decade. In 1954, a national poll revealed that "a whopping 78 percent thought reporting to the FBI neighbors or acquaintances they suspected of being Communists a good idea" (Altschuler 7).

In 2018, A. J. Finn's (Dan Mallory's) novel *The Woman in the Window* (2018) captivated a worldwide audience with its reworking of *Rear Window*. Jefferies has been replaced by a child psychologist named Anna Fox, an agoraphobic woman suffering from depression and a panic disorder. She too has a passion for photography, using a telephoto lens to watch—and vicariously participate in—the lives of people across the street. Since the car accident that killed her family ten months earlier, her only visitors seem to be a psychologist, physical therapist, and the basement tenant who does odd jobs around the house. Instead, she finds companionship in nightly Hitchcock films (and film noir more broadly), imaginary conversations with her deceased husband and child, a temperamental cat, wine, pills, and the internet. One evening she witnesses a murder in a neighbor's house, but the next day, none of it can be proved. No body can be found, and no one believes her. Soon the killer plays a Hitchcock-style game of manipulation and misdirection. He creates a fake persona in a chat room for agoraphobics. He sends her a photograph through an untraceable email account. And he uses her own passwords against her. Like *Rear Window*, Finn's *The Woman in the Window* comments on the dangers of surveillance in American culture. Though the camera still plays a role here, the internet—through Google searches, social media pages, and other online forums—proves to be the real threat. It gives users invasive access into the lives of others only to foster a greater sense of isolation.

Not long after its publication, Tracy Letts adapted *The Woman in the Window* for the screen, and the film is scheduled to be released in 2020. Letts's previous adaptations were based on his own plays, so this film marks a departure for him as a writer. A closer look at the novel provides some insight into the reasons that may have inspired him to work on this project. Certainly, the text's cinematic sensibility lends itself to adaptation. Hitchcock films and other noir murder mysteries act as a type of soundtrack for Anna's life, and her voyeuristic relationship with neighbors speaks to the nature of film itself. As she peers into windows, we peer into her life—and theirs. More significant, Finn's choice to recast *Rear Window* from the perspective of a woman mirrors Letts's interest in powerful female protagonists. Letts is fascinated with women in windows, so to speak—whether commenting on the way others look at them or admiring their ability to gaze out at the mysteries of life. He challenges audiences to recognize the harm of patriarchal oppression, from Dottie's sexual abuse in *Killer Joe* and Mary Page Marlowe's entrapment to Anita's harassment in *Linda Vista*. And his women typically see truths that others, particularly men, cannot.

The novel's preoccupation with lost children and shattered families resonates with Letts's works as well. Agnes and Mary, for instance, carry the pain
of a dead child. Arthur in *Superior Donuts* and Wheeler in *Linda Vista* feel profoundly disconnected from their children. Even Ken's return to Nebraska makes
him realize the distance between himself and his daughters. All of these characters struggle with guilt over these losses and what they perceive to be their
failures as parents and spouses. Anna Fox's marital infidelity led to the fight responsible for the car crash that killed her husband and daughter. Agnes's son was
abducted when she left him unattended in a grocery store for a few minutes.
Mary's divorce—because of her affairs—kept her from her son as he spiraled
into drug addiction. Wheeler's divorce created a similar distance, leaving him
baffled over his son's obsession with pornography, and Arthur's guilt for evad-
ing the draft mirrors his shame for letting his family move away without a fight.

Like so many of these characters, Anna behaves in self-destructive ways to
cope with the pain of loss and alienation. Her alcoholism and drug abuse clearly
share some affinity with the Smith family, Agnes, the Westons, and Mary Page
Marlowe. Anna self-medicates like Violet. She drinks copious amounts of alcohol, and like Mary, her blood alcohol level shocked police at "three times the
legal limit" (179). Anna also feels profoundly alone, linking her agoraphobia
to her social isolation. "I am locked in. I am locked out," she laments when
considering the way others view her (236). Much like Agnes, Anna hopes that
piecing together a mystery will make her important—a "hero . . . a sleuth"
(236)—but the crime across the street only affirms the extent of her marginalization. She has no friends to call from the hospital. Most of the people who
visit her, such as her physical therapist and handyman tenant, are paid to do
so. And she engages in only phantom phone calls with her dead husband and
daughter. Most of Letts's characters experience a similar sense of isolation.
Agnes, Arthur, and Beverly and Violet Weston have locked themselves up, hid-
ing from the world in a motel room, decaying donut shop, and neglected house
respectively. Mary Page Marlowe feels alienated from herself, always performing roles that mask her true self. And Wheeler meets Minnie on the night when
his loneliness drives him out of his apartment: "I thought I'd better get out and
be around other people for a change or I might eat a gun."

One important difference between *The Woman in the Window* and Letts's
plays involves class. Anna differs from many of Letts's characters because of
her wealth, which presumably comes from her years as a professional psychologist and from shared income with her husband. She owns a five-level brown-
stone, and several characters comment on the size and grandeur of it, which
she used to consider the "best-looking house on the block" (166). Just as she
does not balk at the expense of things, her memories of parties and skiing

vacations offer glimpses into an upper- or upper-middle class life. She has never experienced the violent poverty of a trailer park, a seedy motel room, or a bookie trying to collect a debt. She doesn't find herself without a place to stay, like Minnie, nor does she share Anita's fear of losing a "shit job" in *Linda Vista*. Her home may be falling into disrepair ("We aged, the house and I. We've decayed" [167]), but like the Westons, this deterioration comes from addiction and fractured family. It comes from emotional, not financial, hardship.

Another notable difference between the novel and Letts's oeuvre involves race. Anna's neighborhood offers no hints of Harlem's history as the center of African American arts and culture and as a hub of social activism during the Harlem Renaissance and the civil rights movement. In fact, Finn's depiction of Harlem—even this snapshot of gentrified Harlem—shows little evidence of racial diversity. It resembles the cast of Hitchcock's *Rear Window* more than contemporary New York City. A Japanese family lives across the street from Anna, but the only black person to be found is Detective Little. His body and skin tone is an ongoing source of fascination for Anna: "he's holy-shit vast, a mountain of a man: blue-black skin, boulder shoulders, a broad range of chest, a scrub of thick dark hair" (158). At times, it's difficult to determine whether her fascination with his body is about sexual desire or racial othering, but her eroticization of him suggests a degree of discomfort and unfamiliarity. Anna's world—despite living in Harlem—does not include African Americans. She even speculates that her elderly neighbor would certainly view Detective Little through the lens of racism: "I wonder if the neighbors are watching. I wonder if Mrs. Wasserman has just seen an economy-size black man drag me into my house. I bet she's calling the cops right now" (170). This critique of her neighbor may be true (the reader has no way of knowing), but it does reveal Anna's own biases as well. It is also worth noting that Detective Little may, in fact, be the gentlest, kindest police officer in the history of the NYPD. A family man with four kids, he does not raise his voice. He encourages Anna to call him day or night, and he responds to her needs with tireless patience. All the toughness and grit expected of a hardened New York City police officer falls on his female partner. Finn's New York City is a place where gender and racial hierarchies don't exist, where homosexuality is accepted without question, and where ex-cons are reliable handymen. The only thing that spoils this utopia is a pesky teenage psychopath.

The novel's heavy-handedness in avoiding stereotyped portraits of Detective Little as an angry black man or of female officers lacking the toughness of their male counterparts not only remains untrue to the nuanced complexity of human nature, but it also lacks the intentionality driving Letts's portrait of ethnicity in America. Minnie's every gesture in *Linda Vista* is designed to undercut any reading of her as an "Asian flower." Her use of Vietnamese heritage and language offers one example of the way Letts's plays challenge the kind of white privilege that Wheeler and Finn's Anna share. The legacy of racism against Native Americans undergirds the familial trauma in *August: Osage County* as well as the political machinations that hide the ugly truth about Big Cherry in *The Minutes*. Franco and Arthur recognize the need to discuss and do something about racism in America. As Arthur's history with civil rights activism suggests, the realities of racial inequity should not be glossed over or rendered invisible as they are in the world of *The Woman in the Window*. Even Ken's life in Nebraska offers a glimpse into the way racial segregation limits the understanding and empathy of whites.

Finally, Finn anchors the damaged body *The Woman in the Window* in the tradition of *Rear Window*. Jefferies' disability is temporary. His broken legs will heal, and he will learn to pass the time without binoculars. Anna's body seems less damaged from the accident than from her drinking, and similar to her agoraphobia, both are presented as obstacles that she can overcome. Stepping outside thus becomes a clear image for the steps she needs to take to heal from the trauma of losing her family. The bodies of Letts's characters show damage—some lasting, some temporary—and they always comment on either personal or social limitations. Dottie's affinity with Faulkner's Darl and Williams's Laura criticizes the stigmas associated with disability, rejecting the audience's temptation to read her metaphorically. Letts returns to this theme in *The Minutes* through the callous rejection of Mr. Hanratty's project to build a town fountain that is wheelchair accessible. Other times, Letts wants us to consider the symbolic significance of the damaged body. Violet's cancer of the mouth represents the verbal meanness that has eaten away at her family—from the suicide of her husband to her estranged children. Wheeler's deteriorating hip is emblematic of his failures to view women and nonwhites as equals. It also suggests that abandoning photography—art—has left him with a wound that needs to be healed. Franco's missing fingers in *Superior Donuts*, Chris's beaten body in *Killer Joe*, and Mary Page Marlowe's injuries after her DUI signal personal failings and irresponsibility. At the same time, these bodies highlight the forces—whether socioeconomic, racial, or gendered—that damage people.

Ultimately, Letts does not just invite audiences to look through the windows of the Weston house or the Smith's trailer or Wheeler's furnished apartment or the Big Cherry town council meeting. He invites us to look out at the social and cultural context that has shaped these characters. He invites us to consider the ways their lives reveal greater truths about American life. And he implicates all of us in this quest for selfhood and for achieving a society defined by dialogue, community, and shared responsibility.

NOTES

Chapter 1: Understanding Tracy Letts

1. See Kruse.
2. Qtd. in Kruse.
3. See Kruse.
4. See Friedkin.
5. See Friedkin and Kruse.
6. Qtd. in Evans.
7. Qtd. in Kenber.
8. Ibid.
9. Qtd. in Mayer, 181.
10. Ibid, 192–193.
11. Ibid, 194.
12. Qtd. in Isenberg.
13. Letts first collaborated with Friedkin on the film adaptation of *Bug* in 2006, starring Ashley Judd and Michael Shannon.
14. See Friedkin and Miller.
15. Qtd. in Evans.
16. Qtd. in Butler.
17. Ibid.
18. See Weissmann.
19. Qtd. in Witchel.

Chapter 2: Disability and Poverty in *Killer Joe,* *The Glass Menagerie,* and *As I Lay Dying*

1. Letts has acknowledged his admiration for the writings of fellow Oklahoman Jim Thomson. Certainly, Letts's Killer Joe Cooper shares similarities with the protagonist of Thompson's *The Killer Inside Me* (1952). The novel features a well-spoken Texas sheriff, Lou Ford, with a penchant for clichés, sadomasochistic sexual relationships, and violence. Like Texas lawman Killer Joe Cooper, Ford believes in civility ("Out here you are a man and a gentleman, or you aren't anything" [8]), and rudeness often triggers a ruthless savagery on his part. He first beats the prostitute Joyce after she calls him a "son-of-a-bitch" but not before asking her to mind her language: "Don't call me that . . . Don't do it, ma'am" (10). Killer Joe echoes a similar warning about the same insult: "There's no need for name calling . . . You be polite to me. I'm a guest" (70). The violent

impulses beneath this veneer of social propriety prove central to Letts's commentary about poverty, moral bankruptcy, and prejudice in American culture. See Peterseim.

2. Qtd. in Peterseim.

3. The quintessential "femme fatale" is typically viewed as an evil, opaque woman whose alluring sexuality ensnares and ultimately destroys the men in her life. Scholar Julie Grossman, however, warns against viewing these figures purely in terms of sexuality. She insists that a richer understanding of film noir comes from recognizing the femme fatale as reacting to the social practices and institutions limiting women: "They evince ambition to transgress or transcend conventional female gender roles, and/or the desire to exact richer lives (in terms of experience generally) than poverty or modern middle-class existence affords women" (44).

4. See Horwiatz.

5. Some of this influence can be attributed to Letts's work in the theater at the time. Prior to writing the play, Letts appeared in a production of *The Glass Menagerie* for children, and the title *Killer Joe* clearly alludes to Tom Wingfield's description of himself as "Killer Wingfield": "I'm a hired assassin, I carry a tommy-gun in a violin case! . . . They call me Killer, Killer Wingfield, I'm leading a double-life, a simple, honest warehouse worker by day, by night a *czar* of the *underworld, Mother.* I gamble at casinos . . . My enemies plan to dynamite this place. They're going to blow us all sky-high some night! . . . You ugly—babbling old—*witch*" (24). Though this string of cinematic bombast highlights how boring his own life truly is, the violent imagery of assassination, bashed brains, and explosions points to Tom's potential for violence. He may not hit his mother, but he does abandon her and his sister. He leaves them with no financial security and even without electricity (stealing his mother's money instead of paying the electric bill).

6. According to biographer Joseph Blotner, "On October 25, 1929, the day after panic had broken out on Wall Street, [Faulkner] took one of these sheets, unscrewed the cap from his fountain pen, and wrote at the top in blue ink, 'As I Lay Dying.' Then he underlined it twice and wrote the date in the upper right-hand corner. Faulkner would later speak of 'passing coal in a powerhouse,' a phrase to conjure up a grimy fireman heaving huge shovelfuls into red furnace maws. It was a twelve-hour shift he said, beginning at 6 PM. 'I shoveled coal from the bunker into a wheelbarrow and wheeled it and dumped it where the fireman could put it into the boiler. About 11 o'clock the people would be going to bed, and so it did not take much steam. And so we could rest, the fireman and I. He would sit in a chair and doze. I had invented a table out of a wheelbarrow in the coal bunker, just beyond a wall from where a dynamo ran. It made a deep, constant humming noise. There was no more work to do until about 4 AM, when we would have to clean the fires and get up steam again.' This gave him enough time each night, he later said, so that he 'could write another chapter by about 4 AM" (633–34). He completed the novel in just six weeks without changing a word.

7. "Teratology" was coined by French zoologist Isidore Geoffroy Saint-Hilaire. As Thomson notes in her introduction to *Freakery: Cultural Spectacles of the Extraordinary Body*, "what was once the prodigious monster, the fanciful freak, the strange and subtle curiosity of nature, has become today the abnormal, the intolerable" (4).

8. Qtd. in Shakespeare, 197.

9. See Longmore and Umanski, 10.

10. David Kaplan has recently examined the efforts of Chicago theater critics Claudia Cassidy and Ashton Stevens who championed the play, preventing it from closing

and helping Williams "build a reputation as an unusual talent, someone and something worth paying attention to, someone exceptional" (77).

11. Joseph Blotner notes that Faulkner's position at the time was "a supervisory one, with two Negroes to do the labor he later arrogated to himself, but it apparently involved principally his just being there. His wife recalled that he would go to work after dinner, immaculate, and return before breakfast, still immaculate" (634).

12. As Fox has persuasively stated, Laura's nickname for Jim, "Freckles," offers "a gentle reminder . . . that he is her equal; he, too, lives in a contingent body, one that is at once different (marked as it is) and ordinary (what could be more prosaic than freckles?)" (147). Jim's freckles thus underscore Williams's message about the need for a social framework that acknowledges and celebrates the bodily variation among all of us.

13. It is easy to imagine Dottie as one of Amanda's magazine customers in *The Glass Menagerie,* renewing subscriptions to read stories about women with "delicate cupcake breasts, slim, tapering waists, rich, creamy thighs" (19).

14. See Matheou and Billington.

Chapter 3: Conspiracy Theories and Lost Children in *Bug* and *The X-Files*

1. For Timothy Melley, this alienation stems from "agency panic"—the fear that external forces or agents control the individual. As he explains, "paranoia and anxiety about human agency . . . are all part of the paradox in which a supposedly individualist culture conserves its individualism by continually imagining it to be in imminent peril" (6).

2. Such a sentiment has been echoed by a range of scholars. Charles Soukup, for example, notes that Mulder and Scully work for the very government they seek to expose, enabling the audience of *The X-Files* "to playfully resist governmental corruption . . . [while maintaining] the desire for the system to correct itself" (23). Likewise, Stephanie Kelley-Romano observes that "it is easier . . . for people to blame a governmental conspiracy for low wages than it is to contemplate complex theories concerning economic restructuring" (117).

3. Science fiction, another genre whose conventions *Bug* and *The X-Files* deploy, shares a similar interest in economic inequity and exploitation. According to M. Keith Booker, science fiction films have been "particularly pointed in their critique of corporate capitalism" (267), and this preoccupation continues to inspire a range of Marxist readings. Istvan Csicsery-Ronay, for example, has argued that the utopian vision of much science fiction, which "[imagines] progressive alternatives to the status quo," shares an affinity with "the Marxist utopian and social imagination" (113). Carl Freedman likewise notes that "There is much in the transformative thrust of SF that is strongly allied to the spirit of Marxism" (122). And similar sentiments underscore the approach to Ewa Mazierska and Alfredo Suppia's collection *Red Alert: Marxist Approaches to Science Fiction Cinema,* which positions science fiction as an outlet for "resisting the onslaught of capitalism and its ideology" (7).

4. The U.S. Army Chemical Corp's experiments at the Edgewood Arsenal stemmed from concerns about the future of biochemical warfare. At this facility, the military tested chemical weapons such as mustard gas, sarin, LSD, and PCP on American soldiers into the mid-1970s. See Khatchadourian.

Various government agencies secretly tested the impact of drugs and disease on the body as well. The CIA's Project MKUltra, for instance, ran between 1953 and 1973 to study the way drugs could facilitate hypnosis, produce amnesia, induce shock, cause paralysis, and help one withstand torture. Many of the unwitting test subjects included "drug-addicted prisoners, marginalized sex workers, and terminal cancer patients" (Eschner). The 1970s also saw the end of the Tuskegee Experiment. Between 1932 and 1972, the U.S. Public Health Service studied the effects of syphilis on roughly "six hundred sick, desperately poor sharecroppers in Macon County, Alabama" (Washington 157). The agency promised free health care to these infected African American men but actually withheld treatment in order to study the progression of the disease over a forty-year period. Ultimately, it hoped the study would affirm their assumption that the disease affected blacks differently than whites.

5. For Christy Burns, the space alien "operates as a thinly disguised anxiety about illegal aliens who cross national borders, allegedly abduct jobs, and create 'mutant children' through miscegenation" (197). In Gellar's reading of "Fresh Bones," she notes that the episode recalls the real events of the Haitian refugee crisis: the unconstitutional imprisonment by the United States of Haitians, said to be HIV positive though most were falsely diagnosed, held at Guantanamo Bay in the early 1990s. This episode ultimately holds the military leader of what is essentially Guantanamo Bay culpable for profound xenophobic violence—violence explicitly referencing the history of slavery" (35). For Kellner, the depiction of race in *The X-Files* is more ambiguous and problematic: "*The X-Files'* use of images of the occult and its monster figures are thus politically ambiguous, sometimes used to criticize dominant U.S. government or business policies and practices, and sometimes to demonize native peoples and cultures" (217).

6. According to Soukup, "Demographically, viewers of *The X-Files* are upper middle class, white Americans. In fact, the Nielsen company ranked *The X-Files* as the top rated prime-time show for $75,000-plus income homes ('Nielsen Ratings,' 1998). Increasing ratings, a devoted fan-base, and an ideal demographic audience (i.e., affluent, upwardly mobile consumers with disposable income) led to a record setting $1.5 million per episode syndication deal with the cable network FX (Dempsey, 1998)" (15).

Chapter 4: Food, Culinary Justice, and Native American Identity in *August: Osage County*

1. Qtd. in Elvis Mitchell.

2. Letts's allusions to these and other works have inspired a number of comparative analyses. For example, Elizabeth Fifer examines failed parenthood in *August: Osage County* and Eugene O'Neill's *Long Day's Journey into Night,* and Konstantinos Blatanis puts Letts's play in dialogue with the writings of Sam Shepard and Richard Greenberg.

3. As LaDuke notes, "the scorched earth policy and commodity foods program of the 19th century set the stage for the diabetes epidemic in the 20th. The high starch, sugar, and fat content in commodity foods caused high blood sugar levels . . . Prior to the 1940s, there is little record of diabetes in most Native communities. In contrast, it is now the second most common diagnosis for Native Americans admitted to the hospital. By the end of the twentieth century, one in eight Native Americans had diabetes, a rate that is twice that of the non-Indian population" (194–95).

4. Gaye Poole's *Reel Meals, Set Meals: Food in Film and Theatre,* for example, helped carve out a space for food theater studies, noting the importance of food as a "conveyor of meaning" on emotional, psychological, and social levels (3). Just as "food and eating may function as a code, a sign system, a leitmotif of fascinating complexity, to expand the possible repertoire or readings of a play, performance, or film," it can be

"utilized as a means of establishing power differentials between characters, thereby creating strategies for character control and conflict" (4, 48). For Poole, food in the theater has the power to reveal truths about identity and belonging. More recent food studies scholarship, such as Jennifer Packard's *A Taste of Broadway: Food in Musical Theatre,* echoes this sentiment: "Food can be used as shorthand in musical theater to demonstrate, discuss, or dispute the identity of a character . . . Food is often used to indicate participation in a certain group, as well as to show distance between groups" (59).

5. Qtd. in Osenlund.

6. With the consolidation of the meatpacking industry, the implementation of massive feedlots, and the use of assembly line production at slaughterhouses, ground beef became increasingly unsafe in the late twentieth century. Cattle in feedlots typically received little exercise and lived in filth, standing in mounds of manure all day long. The high cost of grain also inspired the meatpacking industry to alter the animals' natural diet. In the United States, seventy-five percent were suddenly being fed livestock waste—"the rendered remains of dead sheep and dead cattle—until August 1997" (Schlosser 202). Cows were also fed dead cats, dead dogs, old newspapers, sawdust, and the waste product of chickens. This diet and these conditions made cattle particularly susceptible to disease, which could be passed along to consumers. Today, seventy-five percent of a cow's diet consists of corn, which makes cattle highly susceptible to ailments such as pneumonia, coccidiosis, and feedlot polio. As Michael Pollan explains, "this unnaturally rich diet of corn that undermines a steer's health fattens his flesh in a way that undermines the health of the humans who will eat it. The antibiotics these animals consume with their corn at this very moment are selecting . . . new strains of resistant bacteria that will someday infect us and withstand the drugs we depend on to treat that infection" (81). The same industry that has implemented processes to maximize profits and fuel demand, in other words, contributes to a number of modern health epidemics.

7. Qtd. in Osenlund.

Chapter 5: *Mary Page Marlowe* and the Patchwork of Personal Identity

1. See Evans and "Tracy Letts on *Mary Page Marlowe*." Steppenwolf Theatre Video. 15 April 2016. https://www.youtube.com/watch?v=BRaf6SRcHTk.

2. Qtd. in Parsi.

3. In *Embodying American Slavery in Contemporary Culture,* Lisa Woolfork discusses the way Perry's novel *Stigmata* (1998) links "quilting aesthetics with trauma theory to know the slave past" (47).

4. "Honoring Zora: Stitching Wise Words, Art Quotes and Art Quilts" was an exhibit of original quilts inspired by the words of Hurston in Charleston, South Carolina. http://blackthreads.blogspot.com/2010/04/honoring-zora-stitching-wise-words-art.html. For more on "The Soul of Zora: A Literary Legacy Through Quilts Exhibition" at Tuskegee University's Legacy Museum in 2019, see http://alabama200.org/media/press/the-soul-of-zora.

5. Quilting has also been used as a compelling metaphor for the collaborative process of the theater. In describing her experiences with the production of *Brief Encounters,* a play addressing homophobia and bullying in schools, for example, Carly Halse describes the "quilting bee" ethos of the group: "By using a democratic process, participants can, from the tangled threads and scraps of historiography and knowledge offered by each individual, vote which pieces they would like to sew into a final product" (28).

Chapter 6: Troubled Masculinity and Aging White Men in
Linda Vista, Superior Donuts, and *Man from Nebraska*

1. As Michael Kimmel explains, "What all men's liberationists promised was that by rejecting traditional masculinity, men would live longer, happier, and healthier lives, lives characterized by close and caring relationships with children, with women, and with other men" (*Manhood,* 284).

2. See Eve Sedgwick's *Between Men: English Literature and Male Homosocial Desire.*

3. For an overview of some of the resistance to the early men's movement, see Rachel Adams and David Savran's discussion of the mythopoetic men's movement and Robert Bly (5).

4. Interestingly, masculinity studies has been remiss in discussing age as an important component of male identity. As Hobbs notes, this field has typically "proposed a homogenized view of manhood," neglecting the impact of aging and different life stages on personal identity. She goes on to argue that the fiction of Philip Roth, Don DeLillo, Jonathan Franzen, and others captures the ambiguities, compromises, and possibilities characterizing the lives of men in their sixties (*Aging,* xiv, 148).

5. In an interview about *Linda Vista,* the lead actor, Ian Barford, discusses the significant revisions to the play between the Chicago and Los Angeles productions: "The rewrites for this iteration of the play are extensive. It doesn't feel like a remount, but rather a new production" (Kaan).

6. See Bazer.

7. Qtd. in Lunden.

8. See Stevens.

9. Likewise, the reference to Ken's high school janitor, who could be either Native or African American, highlights both the lower-class status of nonwhite people in his hometown and his broader indifference about the various histories of racial injustice in the United States.

WORKS CITED

Plays by Tracy Letts

Killer Joe. New York: Theatre Communications Group, 2014.

Bug. New York: Dramatists Play Service, 2005.

Man from Nebraska. Evanston, Il: Northwestern University Press, 2006.

August: Osage County. New York: Dramatists Play Service, 2009.

Superior Donuts. New York: Dramatists Play Service, 2010.

Three Sisters (adaptation of Anton Chekhov). New York: Theatre Communications Group, 2016.

Mary Page Marlowe. New York: Theatre Communications Group, 2016.

Linda Vista

The Minutes

Secondary Sources

Adams, Rachel, and David Savran. "Introduction." *The Masculinity Studies Reader.* Ed. Rachel Adams and David Savran. Malden, MA: Blackwell Publishing, 2002. 1–8.

Altschuler, Glenn C. *All Shook Up: How Rock 'n' Roll Changed America*. Oxford: Oxford University Press, 2003.

American Psychological Association Guidelines for the Psychological Practice with Boys and Men. August 2018. https://pro.psychcentral.com/wp-content/uploads/2019/01/boys-men-practice-guidelines.pdf.

Arnold, Gordon B. *Conspiracy Theory in Film, Television, and Politics*. Westport, CT: Praeger, 2008.

Bano, Tim. "*Killer Joe* Starring Orlando Bloom—Review at Trafalgar Studios, London—'An Unpleasant Revival of a Nasty Play.'" *The Stage* 4 June 2018. https://www.the stage.co.uk/reviews/2018/killer-joe-review-starring-orlando-bloom-trafalgar-studios-london-unpleasant-revival-nasty-play/.

Barkun, Michael. *A Culture of Conspiracy: Apocalyptic Visions in Contemporary America*. Berkeley, CA: University of California Press, 2013.

Bazer, Mark. "Tracy Letts" *The Interview Show*. KPBS, 25 January 2018. https://video.kpbs.org/video/tracy-letts-interview-show-rttitf/.

Berkowitz, Edward. *Something Happened: A Political and Cultural Overview of the Seventies*. New York: Columbia University Press, 2005.

Bigsby, Christopher. *Twenty-First Century American Playwrights*. Cambridge: Cambridge University Press, 2017.

————. "Entering *The Glass Menagerie*." *The Cambridge Companion to Tennessee Williams*. Ed. Matthew C. Roudané. New York: Cambridge University Press, 1997. 29–44.

Billington, Michael. "*Killer Joe* Review: Orlando Bloom's Hitman-Cop Is Queasily Gripping." *The Guardian* 4 June 2018. https://www.theguardian.com/stage/2018/jun/04/killer-joe-review-orlando-bloom-tracy-letts-trafalgar-studios-london.

Blatanis, Konstantinos. "The Value of the Tragic in Contemporary American Drama: Richard Greenberg's *Three of Rain,* Sam Shepard's *The Late Henry Moss,* and Tracy Letts's *August: Osage County.*" *Journal of Contemporary Drama in English* 2.2 (2014): 242–59.

Blotner, Joseph. *Faulkner: A Biography*. New York, Vintage, 1991.

Booker, M. Keith. *Alternate Americas: Science Fiction Film and American Culture*. Westport, CT: Praeger, 2006.

Bray, Robert. "Introduction." *The Glass Menagerie*. 1945. New York: New Directions, 1999. vii–xv.

Brod, Harry. "The Case for Men's Studies" *The Making of Masculinities: The New Men's Studies*. Ed. Harry Brod. London: Allen and Unwin, 1987. 39–62.

Brulotte, Ronda L., and Michael Di Giovine. "Introduction: Food and Foodways as Cultural Heritage." *Edible Identities: Food as Cultural Heritage*. Ed. Ronda L. Brulotte and Michael Di Giovine. New York: Routledge, 2016. 1–28.

Burns, Christy L. "Erasure: Alienation, Paranoia, and the Loss of Memory in *The X-Files*." *Camera Obscura* 45 15.3 (2001): 195–225.

Butler, Isaac. "A Mostly Truthful Interview." *Slate* 2 February 2018. https://slate.com/culture/2018/02/tracy-letts-on-lady-bird-the-post-and-his-new-play-the-minutes.html.

Byrne, Malcolm. *Iran-Contra: Reagan's Scandal and the Unchecked Abuse of Presidential Power*. Lawrence, KS: University Press of Kansas, 2014.

Cantor, Paul A. *Gilligan Unbound: Pop Culture in the Age of Globalization*. New York: Rowman and Littlefield, 2001.

Cave, Alfred A. *Sharp Knife: Andrew Jackson and the American Indians*. Westport, CT: Praeger, 2017.

Chansky, Dorothy, and Ann Folino. "Introduction: Culinary Theatres." *Food and Theatre on the World Stage*. Ed. Dorothy Chansky and Ann Folino. New York: Routledge, 2016. 1–18.

Chansky, Dorothy. *Kitchen Sink Realisms: Domestic Labor, Dining, and Drama in American Theatre*. Iowa City: University of Iowa Press, 2015.

Chaudhuri, Uni. "Bug Bytes: Insects, Information, and Interspecies Theatricality" *Theatre Journal* 65.3 (October 2013): 321–34.

"Chimera." *The X-Files,* season 7, episode 16, FOX, 2 April 2000.

Choate, E. Teresa. "*August: Osage County*." *Theatre Journal* 61.1 (2009): 105–6.

"Closure." *The X-Files,* season 7, episode 11, FOX, 13 February 2000.

Coale, Samuel Chase. *Paradigms of Paranoia: The Culture of Conspiracy in Contemporary American Fiction*. Tuscaloosa: University of Alabama Press, 2004.

Connell, R. W. *Masculinities*. Berkeley: University of California Press, 1995.

Cooper, Lydia. *Masculinities in the Literature of the American West*. New York: Palgrave, 2016.

Counihan, Carole M., and Penny Van Esterik. "Why Food? Why Culture? Why Now?: Introduction to the Third Edition." *Food and Culture: A Reader*. Ed. Carole M. Counihan and Penny Van Esterik. New York: Routledge, 2013. 1–18.

Csicsery-Ronay, Istvan. "Marxist Theory and Science Fiction." Ed. Edward James and Farah Mendelsohn. *The Cambridge Companion to Science Fiction*. Cambridge: Cambridge University Press, 2003. 113–24.

David, Deborah S., and Robert Brannon, ed. *The Forty-Nine Percent Majority: The Male Sex Role*. Reading, MA: Addison-Wesley, 1976.

Davidson, Michael. *Concerto for the Left Hand: Disability and the Defamiliar Body*. Ann Arbor: University of Michigan Press, 2008.

Davis, Lennard J. "Introduction: Disability, Normality, and Power." *The Disability Studies Reader*. Fifth Edition. Ed. Lennard J. Davis. New York: Routledge, 2017. 1–14.

Deacon, Deborah. *War Imagery in Women's Textiles: An International Study of Weaving, Knitting, Sewing*. Jackson, NC: McFarland, 2014.

"Drive." *The X-Files*, season 6, episode 2, FOX, 15 November 1998.

"Duane Barry." *The X-Files*, season 2, episode 5, FOX, 14 October 1994.

Eliot, T. S. "The Hollow Men." 1925. *Collected Poems, 1909-1962*. New York: Faber and Faber, 2002. 79–82.

Eschner, Kat. "What We Know About the CIA's Midcentury Mind-Control Project." *Smithsonian.com* 13 April 2017. https://www.smithsonianmag.com/smart-news/what-we-know-about-cias-midcentury-mind-control-project-180962836/.

Evans, Suzy. "Life After *August:* Tracy Letts and Anna D. Shapiro in Conversation." *American Theatre* 9 March 2016. https://www.americantheatre.org/2016/03/09/life-after-august-tracy-letts-and-anna-d-shapiro-in-conversation/.

"Fallen Angel." *The X-Files*, season 1, episode 10, FOX, 19 November 1993.

Faulkner, William. *As I Lay Dying*. 1930. Ed. Michael Gorra. Norton Critical Editions. New York: Norton, 2010.

Fenster, Mark. *Conspiracy Theories: Secrecy and Power in American Culture*. 2nd Edition. Minneapolis: University of Minnesota Press, 2008

Fifer, Elizabeth. "Memory and Guilt: Parenting in Tracy Letts's *August: Osage County* and Eugene O'Neill's *Long Day's Journey Into Night*." *The Eugene O'Neill Review* 34.2 (2013):183–97.

Finn, A. J. *The Woman in the Window*. New York: William Morrow, 2018.

"Folie à Deux." *The X-Files*, season 5, episode 19, FOX, 10 May 1998.

Fonesca, Marco. *Gramsci's Critique of Civil Society: Towards a New Concept of Hegemony*. New York: Routledge, 2016.

Fox, Ann M. "Reclaiming the Ordinary Extraordinary Body: Or, The Importance of *The Glass Menagerie* for Literary Disability Studies." *Disability Theatre and Modern Drama: Recasting Modernism*. Ed. Kirsty Johnston. New York: Bloomsbury, 2016. 129–52.

———. "'But Mother—I'm—crippled!': Tennessee Williams, Queering Disability, and Dis/Membered Bodies in Performance." *Gendering Disability*. Ed. Bonnie G. Smith and Beth Hutchison. New Brunswick, NJ: Rutgers University Press, 2004. 233–52.

Freedman, Carl. "Marxism and Science Fiction." *Reading Science Fiction*. Ed. James Gunn, Marleen S. Barr, and Matthew Candelaria. New York: Palgrave, 2009. 120–32.

Friedkin, William. "Tracy Letts." *Vanity Fair* January 2014. https://www.vanityfair.com/hollywood/2014/01/tracy-letts-august-osage-county.

Garnier, Caroline. "Temple Drake's Rape and the Myth of the Willing Victim." *Faulkner and Sexualities*. Ed. Annette Trefzer and Ann J. Abadie. Jackson: University Press of Mississippi, 2007. 164–83.

Gellar, Teresa L. *The X-Files (TV Milestones Series)*. Detroit, MI: Wayne State University Press, 2016.

Glaspell, Susan. *Trifles*. 1916. *The Project Gutenberg Ebook of Plays*. https://www.gutenberg.org/files/10623/10623-h/10623-h.htm#TRIFLES.

Gramsci, Antonio. *Selections from the Prison Notebooks*. Ed. and Trans. Quintin Hoare and Geoffrey Nowell Smith. New York: International Publishers, 1971.

Grossman, Julie. *Rethinking the Femme Fatale in Film Noir: Ready for Her Close-Up*. New York: Palgrave McMillan, 2009.

Hagood, Taylor. *Faulkner, Writer of Disability*. Baton Rouge: Louisiana State University Press, 2014.

Halse, Carly. "Brief Encounters Between Disciplines and Cultures: An Analysis of the Dramaturgical Quilting Bee." *Staging Social Justice: Collaborating to Create Activist Theatre*. Ed. Norma Bowles and Daniel-Raymond Nadon. Carbondale: Southern Illinois University Press, 2013. 26–36.

Hanson, Marin F. "Introduction: American Quilts in the Modern Age, 1870–1940." *American Quilts in the Modern Age, 1870–1940: The International Quilt Study Center Collections*. Ed. Marin F. Hanson and Patricia Cox Crews. Lincoln: University of Nebraska Press, 2009. 1–18.

Harrison, Colin. *American Culture in the 1990s*. Edinburg: Edinburg University Press, 2010.

"Hell Money." *The X-Files*, season 3, episode 19, FOX, 29 March 1996.

Hermitosis. "Interview: Pulitzer-Winner Tracy lets Explains Why *Bug* Deserves Another Look." May 12, 2008. http://hermitosis.blogspot.com/2008/05/pulitzer-winner-tracy-letts-on-his.html.

Hilts, Philip J. "Gulf War Syndrome: Is It a Real Disease?" *New York Times* 22 November 1993. https://www.nytimes.com/1993/11/23/science/gulf-war-syndrome-is-it-a-real-disease.html.

Hobbs, Alex. *Aging Masculinity in the American Novel*. New York: Rowan Littlefield, 2016.

———. "Masculinity Studies and Literature." *Literature Compass* 10.4 (2013): 383–95.

Hofstadter, Richard. "The Paranoid Style of American Politics." *The Paranoid Style of American Politics and Other Essays*. Chicago: University of Chicago Press, 1979. 3–40.

Holmberg, Arthur. *David Mamet and the American Macho*. Cambridge: Cambridge University Press, 2012.

Horwiatz, Simi. "Face to Face: Playwright Tracy Letts *Killer Joe:* The Trailer Park in Soho." *Backstage* (November 1998): 15, 48.

Isenberg, Barbara. "Tracy Letts Knows Where to Mine Laughs: Wherever Men Are Behaving Badly." *Los Angeles Times* 9 January 2019. https://www.latimes.com/entertainment/arts/la-ca-cm-tracy-letts-20190109-story.html.

Isherwood, Charles. "*Mary Page Marlowe* Traces a Woman's Evolution in Phases and Fragments." *New York Times* 17 April 2016. https://www.nytimes.com/2016/04/18/theater/review-mary-page-Marlowe-traces-a-womans-evolution-in-phases-and-fragments.html.

Johnston, Kirsty. *Disability Theatre and Modern Drama: Recasting Modernism*. New York: Bloomsbury, 2016.

Kaan, Gil. "Interview: *Linda Vista*'s Ian Barford Muses on Tracy Letts and Steppenwolf." *Broadway World* 16 January 2019. https://www.broadwayworld.com/los

-angeles/article/BWW-Interview-LINDA-VISTAs-Ian-Barford-Muses-on-Tracy-Letts
-Steppenwolf-20190116.

Kaplan, David. "Rescuing *The Glass Menagerie.*" *Tenn at One Hundred: The Reputation of Tennessee Williams.* East Brunswick, NJ: Hansen Publishing, 2011. 61–78.

Kelley-Romano, Stephanie. *Trust No One: The Conspiracy Genre on American Television Southern Communication Journal* 73.2 (April–June 2008): 105–121.

Kellner, Douglas. "*The X-Files* and Conspiracy: A Diagnostic Critique." *Conspiracy Nation: The Politics of Paranoia in Postwar America.* Ed. Peter Knight. New York: New York University Press, 2002. 205–32.

Kelman, David. *Counterfeit Politics: Secret Plots and Conspiracy Narratives in the Americas.* Lewisburg: Bucknell University Press, 2012.

Kenber, Ben. "Tracy Letts Looks Back on *Bug* at New Beverly Cinema." *The Ultimate Rabbit.* 16 August 2016. https://theultimaterabbit.com/2016/08/16/tracy-letts-looks
-back-on-bug-at-new-beverly-cinema/.

Kent, Deborah. "In Search of a Heroine: Images of Women with Disabilities in Fiction and Drama." *Women with Disabilities: Essays in Psychology, Culture, and Politics.* Eds. Michelle Fine and Adrienne Asch. Philadelphia: Temple University Press, 1988. 90–110.

Khatchadourian, Raffi. "Primary Sources: Operation Delirium." *The New Yorker* 12 December 2012: https://www.newyorker.com/news/news-desk/primary-sources
-operation-delirium.

Kimmel, Michael. *Angry White Men: American Masculinity at the End of an Era.* New York: Nation Books, 2013.

———. *Manhood in America: A Cultural History.* New York: The Free Press, 1996.

Kleinbard, David. "*As I Lay Dying:* Literary Imagination, the Child's Mind, and Mental Illness." *The Southern Review* (Winter 1986): 51–68.

Knight, Peter. *Conspiracy Culture: From Kennedy to the X Files.* New York: Routledge, 2001.

Koç, Mustafa, Jennifer Sumner, and Tony Winson. "Introduction: The Significance of Food and Food Studies." *Critical Perspectives in Food Studies.* Ed. Mustafa Koç, Jennifer Sumner, and Tony Winson. New York: Oxford University Press, 2012. xi–xiv.

Kochhar-Lindgren, Kanta. "Disability." *Keywords for American Cultural Studies.* Second Edition. Ed. Bruce Burgett and Glenn Hendler. New York: New York University Press, 2014. 81–84.

Kruse, Missy. "Billie and Tracy Letts Talk About Their Award-Winning Literary Careers." *Tulsa People* December 2009. http://www.tulsapeople.com/Tulsa-People
/December-2009/Online-exclusive-Billie-and-Tracy-Letts-talk-about-their-award
-winning-literary-careers/.

Kyvig, David E. *Daily Life in the United States, 1920–1940: How Americans Lived through the "Roaring Twenties" and the Great Depression.* New York: Ivan R. Dee, 2004.

LaDuke, Winona. *Recovering the Sacred: The Power of Naming and Changing.* Cambridge, MA: South End Press, 2005.

Leverich, Lyle. *Tom: The Unknown Tennessee Williams.* New York: Crown, 1995.

Lewis, Victoria Ann. *Beyond Victims and Villains: Contemporary Plays by Disabled Playwrights.* Ed. Victoria Ann Lewis. New York: Theatre Communications Group, 2005.

Limon, John. "Addie in No Man's Land." *Faulkner and War.* Ed. Noel Polk and Ann J. Abadie. Jackson: University Press of Mississippi, 2004. 36–54.

Longmore, Paul K., and Lauri Umanski. "Introduction: Disability History: From the Margins to the Mainstream." *The New Disability History: American Perspectives*. Ed. Paul K. Longmore and Lauri Umanski. New York: New York University Press, 2001. 1–29.

Lunden, Jeff. "'Superior Donuts': Pulitzer Winner Sets Up New Shop." NPR. *All Things Considered*. 1 October 2009. https://www.npr.org/templates/story/story.php?storyId =113345501.

Matheou, Demetrios. "*Killer Joe*: Theater Review." *The Hollywood Reporter* 4 June 2018. https://www.hollywoodreporter.com/review/killer-joe-theater-review-1116728.

Mayer, John. *Steppenwolf Theatre Company of Chicago: In Their Own Words*. New York: Bloomsbury Methuen Drama, 2016.

Mazierska, Ewa, and Alfredo Suppia. "Introduction: Marxism and Science Fiction Cinema." *Red Alert: Marxist Approaches to Science Fiction Cinema*. Ed. Ewa Mazierska and Alfredo Suppia. Detroit: Wayne State University Press 2016. 1–24.

McClure, John A. "Forget Conspiracy: Pynchon, DeLillo, and the Conventional Counterconspiracy Narrative." *Conspiracy Nation: The Politics of Paranoia in Postwar America*. Ed. Peter Knight. New York: New York University Press, 2002. 254–74.

McKinley, Jesse. "Tracy Letts Can't Fight with His Playwright." *New York Times* 26 Feb. 2020. https://www.nytimes.com/2020/02/26/theater/tracy-letts-the-minutes.html.

McKinley, Maggie. *Masculinity and the Paradox of Violence in American Fiction, 1950–1975*. New York: Bloomsbury, 2015.

Melley, Timothy. *Empire of Conspiracy: The Culture of Paranoia in Postwar America*. Ithaca: Cornell University Press, 2000.

Miller, Julie. "Carrie Coon Almost Threw Out Her Wedding Gown" *Vanity Fair* 2017 https://www.vanityfair.com/hollywood/2017/12/carrie-coon-the-post-leftovers -wedding-dress.

Mitchell, David T., and Sharon L. Snyder. *Narrative Prosthesis: Disability and the Dependencies of Discourse*. Ann Arbor: University of Michigan Press, 2000.

Mitchell, Elvis. "Tracy Letts: *August: Osage County*." *The Treatment*. KCRW, Los Angeles, 22 Jan. 2014. https://www.kcrw.com/news-culture/shows/the-treatment/tracy-letts -august-osage-county.

Mohler, Courtney Elkin. "Nostalgia, Irony, and the Re-Emergence of the Reified American Indian Other in *August: Osage County*." *Text & Presentation, 2010 (The Comparative Drama Conference Series, 7)*. Ed. Kiki Gounaridou. Jefferson, NC: McFarland, 2011. 130–42.

Moon, John Ellis van Courtland. "The US Biological Weapons Program." *Deadly Cultures: Biological Weapons Since 1945*. Ed. Mark Wheelis, Lajos Rózsa, and Malcom Dando. Cambridge, MA: Harvard University Press, 2006. 9–26.

Moss, Michael. *Salt Sugar Fat: How the Food Giants Hooked Us*. New York: Random House, 2013.

Newell, Aimee E. *A Stitch in Time: The Needlework of Aging Women in Antebellum America*. Athens, OH: Ohio University Press, 2014.

Opal, J. M. *Avenging the People: Andrew Jackson, the Rule of Law, and the American Nation*. Oxford: Oxford University Press, 2017.

Osenlund, R. Kurt. "Interview: Tracy Letts Talks *August: Osage County*." *Slant Magazine* 19 December 2013. https://www.slantmagazine.com/features/article/interview -tracy-letts/P2.

"Oubliette." *The X-Files*, season 3, episode 8, FOX, 17 November 1995.

Packard, Jennifer. *A Taste of Broadway: Food in Musical Theatre.* New York: Rowman and Littlefield, 2018.

"Paper Hearts." *The X-Files,* season 4, episode 10, FOX, 15 December 1996.

Parsi, Novid. "Tracy Letts on His New Steppenwolf Play and Chicago's 'Talent Drain.'" *Chicago Magazine* 7 March 2016. https://www.chicagomag.com/Chicago-Magazine /March-2016/Tracy-Letts-Mary-Page-Marlowe/.

Peña, Devon G. et al. "Introduction: Mexican Deep Food: Bodies, the Land, Food, and Social Movements." *Mexican-Origin Foods, Foodways, and Social Movements: Decolonial Perspectives.* Ed. Devon G. Peña, et al. Fayetteville: University of Arkansas Press, 2017. xv–xxxiii.

Peterseim, Locke. "Interview: *Killer Joe* Screenwriter and Playwright Tracy Letts." *Hammer and Thump: A Film Blog.* 3 August 2012. http://www.openlettersmonthly .com/hammerandthump/interview-killer-joe-screenwriter-and-playwright-tracy-letts/.

"Pilot." *The X-Files,* season 1, episode 1, FOX, 10 September 1993.

Pleck, Joseph H. *The Myth of Masculinity.* Cambridge, MA: MIT Press, 1981.

Pollan, Michael. *The Omnivore's Dilemma: A Natural History of Four Meals.* New York: Penguin, 2006.

Poole, Gaye. *Reel Meals, Set Meals: Food in Film and Theatre.* Sydney, Australia: Currency, 1999.

"Pusher." *The X-Files,* season 3, episode 17, FOX, 23 February 1996.

"Quick Facts: Osage County, Oklahoma." *Census.gov,* United States Census Bureau, https://www.census.gov/quickfacts/osagecountyoklahoma. Accessed 9 Jan 2020.

Rackin, Donald. "Blessed Rage: The *Alices* and the Modern Quest for Order." *Alice in Wonderland.* 1865. Ed. Donald Gray. Norton Critical Editions. New York: Norton, 2013. 323–330.

Roberts, Paul. *The End of Food.* New York: Mariner, 2009.

Rollings, Willard H. *The Osage: An Ethnohistorical Study of Hegemony on the Prairie-Plains.* Columbia, Missouri: University of Missouri Press, 1992.

Sandahl, Carrie, and Philip Auslander. "Introduction: Disability Studies in Commotion with Performance Studies." *Bodies in Commotion: Disability and Performance.* Ed. Carrie Sandahl and Philip Auslander. Ann Arbor: University of Michigan Press, 2005. 1–12.

Schlosser, Eric. *Fast Food Nation: The Dark Side of the All-American Meal.* New York: Mariner, 2001.

Sedgwick, Eve Kosofsky. *Between Men: English Literature and Male Homosocial Desire.* New York: Columbia University Press, 1985.

"Sein and Zeit." *The X-Files,* season 7, episode 10, FOX, 6 February 2000.

Shakespeare, Tom. "The Social Model of Disability." *The Disability Studies Reader.* Fifth Edition. Ed. Lennard J. Davis. New York: Routledge, 2017. 195–203.

"Shapes." *The X-Files,* season 1, episode 19, FOX, 1 April 1994.

Shaw, Robert. *American Quilts: The Democratic Art, 1780–2007.* New York: Sterling, 2009.

Showalter, Elaine. *Sister's Choice: Tradition and Change in American Women's Writing.* New York: Oxford University Press, 1991.

Soukup, Charles. "Television Viewing as Vicarious Resistance: *The X-Files* and Conspiracy Discourse." *Southern Communication Journal* 68 (2002): 14–26.

Stevens, Beth. "One on One: *Man from Nebraska* Playwright Tracy Letts." *The Broadway Channel* 21 February 2017. https://www.youtube.com/watch?v=YJQsLhddEpM.

"Summer Man." *Mad Men,* season 4, episode 8, AMC, 12 September 2010.

Sundquist, Eric J. *Faulkner: The House Divided.* Baltimore: Johns Hopkins University Press, 1983.

Taylor, Paul. "*Killer Joe,* Trafalgar Studios, London, Review: Orlando Bloom Has Full Command of the Stage—But the Play Itself Is Queasily Dated." *Independent* 5 June 2018 https://www.independent.co.uk/arts-entertainment/theatre-dance/reviews/killer-joe-orlando-bloom-review-theatre-tracy-letts-trafalgar-studios-a8383846.html.

"Teliko." *The X-Files,* season 4, episode 3, FOX, 18 October 1996.

"Theef." *The X-Files,* season 7, episode 14, FOX, 12 March 2000.

Thompson, Jim. *The Killer Inside Me.* 1952. New York: Mulholland Books, 2014.

Thomson, Rosemarie Garland. "Introduction: From Wonder to Error—A Genealogy of Freak Discourse in Modernity." *Freakery: Cultural Spectacles of the Extraordinary Body.* Ed. Rosemarie Garland Thomson. New York: New York University Press, 1996. 1–19.

Twitty, Michael W. *The Cooking Gene: A Journey through African American Culinary History in the Old South.* New York: Amistad, 2017.

Washington, Harriet A. *Medical Apartheid: The Dark History of Medical Experimentation on Black Americans from Colonial Times to the Present.* New York: Doubleday, 2007.

Weissmann, Dan. "A Play About Politics For (But Not About) the Age of Trump." *All Things Considered.* NPR 16 December 2017. https://www.npr.org/2017/12/16/571162369/a-play-about-politics-for-but-not-about-the-age-of-trump.

Wickett, Murray R. *Contested Territory: Whites, Native Americans, and African Americans in Oklahoma, 1865–1907.* Baton Rouge: Louisiana State University Press, 2000.

Williams, Tennessee. *The Glass Menagerie.* 1945. New York: New Directions, 1999.

Wisnicki, Adrian S. *Conspiracy, Revolution, and Terrorism from Victorian Fiction to the Modern Novel.* New York: Routledge, 2007.

Witchel, Alex. "Tracy Letts Still Haunted by Past." *New York Times Magazine* 21 March 2014. https://www.nytimes.com/2014/03/23/magazine/tracy-letts-is-still-haunted-by-his-past.html.

Zlolkowski, Theodore. *Cults and Conspiracies: A Literary History.* Baltimore: John Hopkins University Press, 2017.

INDEX